D0772702

HOLLYWOOD TV AND MOVIE CARS

William Krause

New York to Paris

Firestone

MBI Publishing Company

Dedication

To all the men and women working behind the scenes who helped to bring these cars to life and capture our imaginations.

Acknowledgements

This book and the information and photos in it would not have been possible without the help and cooperation of a great many people who also share an interest in the story behind these wonderful cars and motorcycles. I wish to thank Judy Singer, Pat Kowalski, Leith Adams, Carlos Noriega, and Marion Bachand at Warner Brothers; Howard Mandelbaum and the gang at Photofest; David Kunz, Anthony Bologna, Randy Leffingwell, Leonard Maltin, Dean Jeffries, Tony Thacker, Jim Wangers, John Schinella, Jim Mattison, Mark Hitchins, Jim Benjaminson, and John Gunnell at Old Cars Weekly; Don Keefe, Paul Zazarine, and the Everett Collection; Claire Brandt, Doug Stevenson, David Evans, Eric Dahlquist Sr., Michael Leone, Denice Halicki, and Dave Buchko at BMW; Harry Carlton at Aston Martin Lagonda LTD.; Ken Gross and the Petersen Automotive Museum; countless terrific websites; Keith Mathiowetz, Darwin Holmstrom, and Tom Heffron for making it look good, and finally my wife, Katie, for putting up with the long hours and late nights.

First published in 2001 by MBI Publishing Company, Galtier Plaza, Suit 200, 380 Jackson St., St. Paul, MN 55101-3885, USA

© William Krause, 2001

MBI Publishing Company books are also available at discounts in bulk quantity for industrial or sales-promotional use. For details write to Special Sales Manager at Motorbooks International Wholesalers & Distributors, Galtier Plaza, Suit 200, 380 Jackson St., St. Paul, MN 55101-3885, USA

On the front cover: Four famous car stars, from the top: the 1932 Ford five-window hot rod from *American Graffiti*, the never-damaged 1969 Dodge Charger seen in *The Dukes of Hazzard* television series, James Bond's Aston Martin DB5, and Herbie. *Everett Collection*

On the frontispiece: Actors Van Williams and Bruce Lee pose with *Black Beauty*, the four-wheeled star of *The Green Hornet*. *Everett Collection*

On the title page: Promoting *The Great Race*, Jack Lemmon, Tony Curtis, and Natalie Wood are shown with the *Leslie Special*. *Photofest*

On the back cover: Getty ready for action are *Christine* and *Black Beauty*. *Photofest* In *Gone in 60 Seconds*, Eleanor steals the show with this spectacular record-setting jump. *Denice Halicki Collection*

Library of Congress Cataloging-in-Publication Data Available

ISBN 0-7603-0755-5

Edited by Keith Mathiowetz
Designed by Mark Odegard

Printed in Hong Kong

Contents

Foreword: We're Gonna Put You in the Movies! 6

Introduction 9

CHAPTER 1

The James Bond Aston Martin DB5 "with Modifications" 13
- James Bond's Car • Aston versus Bentley
- Stears' and Adam's Car • The Most Famous Accessory
- The Fate of the Original DB5

CHAPTER 2

James Bond: Beyond British 23
- Bond Turns Japanese • Detroit Does Bond • Bond on a Bike
- Buzzing Hornets, Flying Matadors, and Half-Baked Alliances
- Roger Moore Gets a Real Bond Car • Bond Buys a Beemer

CHAPTER 3

Cops and Robbers 39
- Bullitt • The Italian Job • Gone in 60 Seconds • Smokey and the Bandit

CHAPTER 4

Hot Rods, Hippies, and Hoodlums 57
- Easy Rider • Two-Lane Blacktop • Vanishing Point
- American Graffiti • The California Kid • Corvette Summer

CHAPTER 5

Racing 71
- The Great Race • Grand Prix • Le Mans

CHAPTER 6

Flights of Fancy 86
- Chitty Chitty Bang Bang • The Love Bug • Herbie Rides Again
- Herbie Goes to Monte Carlo • Christine • Back to the Future

CHAPTER 7

TV Cars and Bikes 103
- The Green Hornet • The Monkees • Then Came Bronson • Bearcats!
- Starsky & Hutch • The Dukes of Hazzard • Magnum P.I.

Index 127

Foreword:
We're Gonna Put You In The Movies!
by Eric C. Dahlquist

In 1992, Warner Brothers re-released a remastered collectors' edition of the film classic *Casablanca* as part of a 50th anniversary celebration. I attended the "premiere" in Los Angeles at Grumman Mann's Chinese Theatre. One thing became apparent as soon as *Casablanca's* title sequence rolled across Mann's huge screen: much of the rich detail and nuance of the original Academy Award winner, detail lost in the various edited versions of the highly acclaimed drama shown on television over the past 40 years, resurfaced after half a century. For me, someone who has spent a good part of the last 25 years placing products in motion pictures and television, it was interesting to see the predominance of certain branded products that appear throughout the film.

Most of *Casablanca's* dramatic interplay occurs in Rick's (played by Humphrey Bogart) Café Americain in French Morocco during the early stages of World War II. Since Rick's is a nightclub, it's only natural to see alcohol and drinking. Mostly, the bottle labels are turned away from the camera—with one exception, Mumms Champagne. They drink a lot of champagne in this movie, and it is clear what brand they're using.

Since *Casablanca* was a screen adaptation of an unproduced play called "Everybody Comes to Rick's", there are a lot of close-ups of the lead actors—Humphrey Bogart, Ingrid Bergman, Claude Rains, Paul Henreid, Sidney Greenstreet, Peter Lorre, Conrad Veidt, and Dooley Wilson—and it is apparent several of them are wearing wristwatches. Gruen wristwatches. In one flashback scene, Bogie is sporting the classic and unusual looking Gruen Curvex, a favorite with watch collectors ever since. I mention *Casablanca* because it is one of the best-known films from Hollywood's

Golden Age, when dramatic content was supposedly unsullied by commercialism. At least that's what many of the individuals and agencies, now engaged in the activity of placing products in film and television, commonly believe. This is probably because the "art" of placing products in theatrical production became a professional business science only in the last decade. But, of course, nothing is really new under the sun.

In the case of cars in movies, you can bet many of the recognizable brands have gotten up on the silver screen because somebody made a deal with the producer, director, star, studio marketing person, or whomever to make sure it happened. The first automotive placement I encountered but didn't recognize as such was in the 1971 racing classic *Le Mans*, starring Steve McQueen. I was still editor of *Motor Trend* magazine then, and I went to visit Steve in Solar Productions' office in Studio City, California, for an interview and to talk about how *Le Mans* was going to combine the exciting action of John Frankenheimer's 1966 film *Grand Prix* with the romance of Claude Lelouch's 1966 film *A Man and a Woman*.

Of course, Porsche and Ford played dominant roles in *Le Mans* because they were preeminent in international racing. At the time we met, Steve was focused on getting *Le Mans* finished, but he also had a larger-range view for Solar Productions.

As luck would have it, John Z. DeLorean had just become general manager of Chevrolet in 1970. Once he was offered involvement with the McQueen film, he jumped at the chance to get involved with Hollywood, which DeLorean quite accurately perceived as the ultimate mass awareness and marketing tool. A few years later when

DeLorean was forced out of GM, one of the character faults his peer executives raised was having gone "Hollywood," a definitely suspect direction in Detroit at the time.

I saw DeLorean numerous times in those years, and more than once he expanded on the almost limitless ways a company could use film and television to create mass appeal faster and more dramatically than traditional advertising could ever do. It is perhaps the supreme irony that after his car company had gone bankrupt, the DeLorean automobile would gain immortality in *Back to the Future,* parts I, II, and III.

But if DeLorean and Chevrolet had been premature visionaries in the 1970s, Ford and Packard before them had competed for the spotlight going back to silent films in the 1920s. In fact, it is not that much of a stretch to imagine that some of DeLorean's ideas of Hollywood's promotion potential may have in fact been acquired at Packard when he did a stint as chief engineer at that company during its fading days.

Packard executives, even in the motion picture's infancy, had realized the impact Hollywood was having on the American conscience, and it was no accident stars like Clark Gable, Gary Cooper, Jean Harlow, and a host of others were owners, often through special deals of one kind or another. Additionally, Packard turned up on the silver screen more often than Ford in starring roles, almost always driven by one of the "smart set," which was, after all, only art imitating life. In the 1920s and 1930s, Packard was the hottest luxury car in America, outselling its closest competition, Cadillac, by three-to-one!

At the opposite end of the spectrum, Ford, because of the ubiquitous Model T, had been used by Hollywood before it was Hollywood. But Ford really began coming to prominence during television's "Golden Era" in the 1950s and 1960s on police shows like *Dragnet, The Line Up,* and of course, *The FBI,* in which virtually all the rolling stock—driven by the good guys, bad guys, what have you—ranged from plain-Jane N.D. (non-descript) stakeout cars to T-Birds and Lincoln Continentals. For about five years, Ford completely dominated automotive placement on television. It literally was an embarrassment of riches.

In typical fashion, being late to capitalize on a developing trend, GM had little or no official

Since the earliest films, cars were frequently used as props, particularly in comedies. The Keystone Cops were famous for falling off and dragging behind their paddy wagon while others like Laurel and Hardy destroyed just about every car they drove. *Photofest*

Hollywood involvement until the mid-to-late 1960s, but it really got into gear with DeLorean and Chevrolet. At one point, the bow tie brigade alone had over 400 cars and trucks dedicated to West Coast production. Inevitably, with a large number of vehicles like this, excesses developed and the entire program was deep-sixed after DeLorean departed the scene. That's when the horror stories began to surface. I remember talking to one GM controller at a GMC truck party in the late 1980s, and he went on at length about the fact that the terrific abuses of the Chevy movie program not only cost him many agonizing hours of repossessing cars from starlets and starlets' gardeners, but cost him any advancement for the rest of his GM career.

After several years cool-down at GM to let the bitter memories fade, Pontiac's merchandising manager, Jim Graham, managed to slip ex-stuntman-turned-producer Hal Needham several black Trans Ams for *Smokey and the Bandit,* and the rest is history.

That was about the time I got involved. GMC had been burned in fabricating a couple of

Ford was directly involved with Hollywood from the earliest days of celluloid, providing cars for movies. It is difficult to say Ford was in it for the publicity since most of the cars were destroyed, as was this 1934 sedan from a Three Stooges film. *Old Cars Weekly*

preproduction prototypes of the yet-to-be-announced Class Eight General for *Movin' On*, a truckers' show starring Claude Akins. GMC was GM's vehicle division with the correspondingly smallest advertising budget. They were therefore inclined to perceive product placement as a way to greatly extend the brand reach of their trucks, especially the pickups, for a very attractive investment. They asked my agency, Vista Group, to do some research and build a business case, configuring product placement as a business discipline like public relations or advertising.

Simultaneously, a stroke of good luck befell us. In a striking lapse of judgment, Ford, still by far the dominant vehicle in Hollywood, switched agencies and stopped all activity for six to nine months. This happened precisely in the middle of the film industry's production season and many features and television shows were left holding the bag with no vehicles. As a result of the ensuing turmoil, Ford's move left a bad taste and feeling of betrayal with the film industry, which didn't recede for almost a decade.

We drove smack into the middle of this vehicle void with GMC's new product placement program, and with the help of a very supportive client we were suddenly stars in *Smokey II,* Clint Eastwood's *Every Which Way but Loose, Emergency, Jaws, Rockford Files,* and later *A Team, Hardcastle and McCormick, Dallas,* and *Falcon Crest,* just to name the highlights.

Probably the high-water mark of the 1980s was *Knight Rider,* which simultaneously launched David Hasselhoff's career and the third-generation Pontiac Firebird. In what amounted to a five-year-running commercial for Pontiac, the *Knight Rider* opportunity started innocently enough when one of the show's line producers, Harker Wade, approached me in our church parking lot one Sunday morning after Mass in the spring of 1981.

He said he was working with Glen Larson (*The Fall Guy*) on a new action-adventure show that starred a computerized talking car. A Datsun Z car was written into the original script, but Harker wanted to know if GM had anything hotter coming out that would work in this role. Of course: the all-new Trans Am! Pontiac's general manager, Bill Hoglund, had told me at a meeting just days before that he would like to see his brand-new baby in a James Bond kind of movie or TV show.

Obviously, the zoomie new 1982 Trans Am would be perfect. Just two things stood in the way: production for the car wouldn't start until the late summer, almost too late for filming, and second, some Pontiac managers thought the show's concept was too humorous. I still have a rejection letter comparing the *Knight Rider* car, KITT, to *Francis the Talking Mule* or *My Mother the Car.* They had no clue where automotive electronics was going.

Fortunately, wiser heads prevailed, and with the help of UAW, the GM Van Nuys assembly plant, and a lot of good Pontiac people who wanted to see this happen, the first four black Trans Ams that rolled off the line were driven to a waiting car carrier that whisked them off to the Larson Production set where the crews were literally poised to start shooting.

Home runs in the product placement game only come once in a while, but *Knight Rider* was definitely a bases-loaded shot out of the park in the bottom of the ninth. Over the years I've had more than my share, but win or lose, the product placement business has never been dull.

The opening sequence of the movie *Grand Prix* has been etched in my mind since I first saw the film at the Cooper Theater, one of Minneapolis' finest movie houses, in 1967. To this day it is still one of my favorite big screen auto moments. You can picture it in your mind from the mere mention of it.

The screen is black. Suddenly the sound of an engine roaring to life fills the theater, and as the camera pulls back you realize the lens is actually inside the exhaust pipe of a Formula One car. Shortly thereafter the screen is filled with John Frankenheimer's Academy Award–winning mosaics of blipping throttles and jumping tachometer needles.

The next thing you know you are on board a real Formula One car during a real race through the streets of Monaco. An incredible opening that you can watch over and over again.

It is just one of those memorable moments of cars on the movie screen or the television screen that everyone has. It is one of my favorite scenes but each of us has our own. Perhaps yours was the first time you saw TV's *Batmobile*, or the gadget sequences from James Bond's Aston Martin DB5 in *Goldfinger,* or *Thunderball,* or the cars from *American Graffiti,* or the smirk you got from the outrageous *Munsters* car.

Ever since the invention of the moving picture, cars have played a major role in the history of film. In the earliest days of cinema, automobiles were as interesting as the movies themselves, so cars and car races were frequently featured on screen. Racing made for especially dramatic newsreel footage.

Cars then became comedic props for the slapstick antics of Charlie Chaplin, Buster Keaton, and the Keystone Cops among others. In most cases the stars would be falling out of or dragging behind the cars or end up in some horrible crash where the car was left in pieces.

Even in those early days, Ford recognized the promotional value of having its cars seen by the public. To that end Ford provided cars to Hollywood for use in the movies. The most frightening thing about these films is that most of the stunts involved the actors and stuntmen actually dragging behind a car or crashing it at full speed.

The *Batmobile* is likely the most famous car ever used in any movie or TV show. The car, built by George Barris, was based on the 1955 Lincoln Futura concept car and rocketed to stardom in the TV series' first season. *Everett Collection*

The 1969 Plymouth Barracuda driven by Don Johnson in CBS' *Nash Bridges* is the current example of using a signature car to define a character. This is familiar territory for Johnson who also drove a Ferrari Daytona Spyder replica in the 1980's *Miami Vice*.
Everett Collection

Ford Model Ts were plentiful on film and were regularly destroyed by Laurel and Hardy, Charlie Chaplin, Harold Lloyd, and many others. While W. C. is mostly remembered for his intoxicated quips, he did an incredible job destroying a Duesenberg in the 1940 comedy *The Bank Dick*. The film itself is quite tedious unless you are a real Fields devotee but is worth a look to appreciate the driving skills, along with the fact that a Duesenberg was sacrificed for the film.

As cars and car styling became status symbols, they were also used as props to help define the characters in a film. If they were to be suave and elitist, you would have a car of some status such Rex Harrison's Yellow Rolls-Royce, Robert Shaw's Packard in *The Sting,* or the Darrin-bodied Packard driven by George Peppard who played TV's *Banecek.*

Banecek's Packard was an exception to the rule of most private eyes or undercover cops. You can almost always count on something sporting or dilapidated for this group, like Tom Selleck's Ferrari 308 from *Magnum P.I.* or Don Johnson's Ferrari Daytona Spyder kit car from *Miami Vice.* Johnson has carried that theme over into his new series, *Nash Bridges,* driving a 1971 Plymouth 'Cuda convertible. *Starsky and Hutch* had Starsky's Ford Gran Torino and James Garner got a new Firebird each year in *Rockford Files,* while Don Adams' Maxwell Smart had a Sunbeam Alpine, an

Opel GT, and Volkswagen Karmen Ghia. And of course James Bond had his unforgettable Aston Martins, Lotus, and BMWs.

Playing it the other way was Peter Falk's rumpled Inspector Columbo driving a tatty Peugeot convertible, Robert Blake's *Baretta* in a ratty four-door Chevrolet Impala, and David Jansen was forever begging rides in *Harry O* because his Austin Healey was in a constant state of disrepair.

Then there was the rush of hot rodder and rebel films that centered around the cars. This was a veritable B-movie bonanza with the likes of *Hot Rod, Hot Rod Hullabaloo, Hot Rod Gang, Hot Rod Girl,* and *Hot Rods to Hell.* There is no end to this genre of films, and all provide a great look at period hot rods in action.

The bad-boy biker flicks are a distant second to the hot rods, but there is no shortage of these films and there are, of course, that small handful that really stand out. You have Marlon Brando and his Triumph in *The Wild One,* Joe Namath and Ann Margaret in *C.C. and Company,* and the quintessential *Easy Rider* with Peter Fonda, Dennis

Jessica Tandy and Morgan Freeman pose in front of a 1948 Hudson Hornet from the film *Driving Miss Daisy.* The film featured extensive scenes shot inside the Hudson as well as a variety of Cadillacs. While the cars were not the stars, there was a significant amount of screen-time in and around the cars.

Hopper, and Jack Nicholson. *Then Came Bronson* was TV's rebel biker, but without the edge and angst the series did not last.

Few films have been able to capture the true-life excitement of the racing scene, yet there is no shortage of those that have tried.

You have things like *Dragstrip Girl*, *The Devil's Hairpin*, and *The Green Helmet* from the wonderful B-class. Even Frankie and Annette went to the races in *Fireball 500*, and Elvis was crooning and crashing in *Viva Las Vegas*. If you take your big screen racing more seriously, *The Racers* with Kirk Douglas and *Winning* with Paul Newman are a step up, but nothing holds a candle to Steve McQueen's masterful *Le Mans* for racing action.

The Academy Award–winning *Grand Prix* is filled with phenomenal racing sequences from the 1966 Formula One season, but it gets bogged down in the soap opera–like storyline.

If you are any kind of a car enthusiast you can quickly produce a list of cars that played major or minor roles in TV or the movies. At the top of that list is likely to be the features that had a car as the star. This includes the Volkswagen Beetle from *The Love Bug*, the 1957 Plymouth Fury in *Christine*, the 1977 Pontiac Trans Am in *Smokey and the Bandit*, the DeLorean-based time machine from *Back to the Future*, or the 1928 Porter from *My Mother the Car*. At the bottom of the list might be the Pontiac Safari station wagon that was always parked at the curb on *My Three Sons*, Jack Benny's Maxwell, or the *Partridge Family* bus. Whatever it may be, you have a distinct image of the car, the time, and the film.

I would be willing to bet that if you are reading this book you have watched countless films and television shows just for a glimpse of a car, truck, or motorcycle you saw in the previews.

C'mon, admit it. You have sat through some of the worst stories and most pathetic acting ever recorded on celluloid just to see a car. Case in point: In college my roommate and I stayed home on a Friday night to watch the pilot episode of *Knight Rider* because the commercials showed some exciting sequences with a black Firebird. Needless to say, it did not live up to our car-guy expectations even though the show went on to be a huge hit.

KITT, the car in *Knight Rider*, was essentially a prop, but it quickly became as much the star of the

Author Bill Krause in *Eleanor,* the star of *Gone in 60 seconds.*

show as David Hasselhoff while other cars simply remained props, like Chevy Chase's "Family Truckster" from *National Lampoon's Vacation* and the Chrysler K-car convertible that Steve Martin and John Candy destroy in *Planes, Trains and Automobiles*. Classic moments that you will never forget.

Like Abbott to Costello, Laurel to Hardy, and Carson to McMahon, you have Thomas Magnum and his Ferrari, James Bond and his Aston Martin, and of course Batman and his Batmobile. You cannot have one without the other. It is a chemistry that makes the visual images work and sets the tone for the character. Think of all the TV and movie characters for whom you can name the kind of car they drive or motorcycle they ride. You can come up with quite a list in no time at all.

Finally are the films and shows where the car is the star. The car is the focal point of the story and entire reason you are there to see the show. The automobile in film is as much a cultural phenomenon as the vehicles themselves are in real life. How many inanimate objects have been at the heart of so many films? Cars are as much a part of the movies as they are part of life.

According to Dave Mann and Ron Main's book *Races, Chases and Crashes*, there have been over 500 motor car–related movies and countless television programs. This book is a celebration of all those cars and car films along with some of the lesser-known stories that will give you a grin and take you back to your own first experience with cars on film.

—*Bill Krause*

CHAPTER 1

The James Bond Aston Martin DB5
"with Modifications"

The first James Bond movie produced one of the best and most famous screen introductions in the history of film. It was an introduction that has endured over four decades and 20 films.

Dr. No debuted in 1962 starring Sean Connery as British secret agent 007. We don't immediately meet the world-renowned super spy, however, until the movie takes us to Kingston, Jamaica, to witness two dastardly murders, then back to London for a frenzied search for the man himself by his employers. We don't learn until later that it is 3:00 A.M.

Finally we enter the shimmering private London club Le Cercle, on the heels of an MI6 agent inquiring about Bond. The camera pans the room of formally attired guests for our hero but comes to rest on a stunning woman in a red dress at the baccarat table. Sylvia Trench (Eunice Gayson) is her name and she is repeatedly and rapidly losing money to the faceless gentleman controlling the card shoe. As she secures additional funds, in exasperation she asks her opponent's identity.

Cut to the tuxedo-clad gentleman lighting his cigarette in a cool and casual manner as no one else could as he utters the famous phrase: "Bond" snapping the lighter shut, "James Bond." That instant captured forever the defining look and style of James Bond, the smooth, sophisticated, super-spy created by novelist Ian Fleming.

His series of international espionage capers spawned a monopoly of 20 action-packed films brimming with exotic locations, luscious women, nefarious villains, diabolical schemes of global domination, and incredible peril-thwarting gadgets. Through it all two things have endured: the man and his cars.

James Bond's Car

Outside of the original Batmobile there is no car more famous than Bond's first car, the Silver Birch Aston Martin DB5 "with modifications." It debuted along with its on-screen creator "Q" (Desmond Llewelyn) in the third Bond film, *Goldfinger*, in 1964. Bond's second car, the Lotus Esprit, ranks a distant second. It first appeared with Connery's successor Roger Moore in *The Spy Who Loved Me* in 1977. Similar to the DB5 premiere, the Lotus was introduced in Moore's third Bond film.

The Lotus was a worthy car for Bond and fitting for the 1970s-styled Bond created by Moore. Many credible gadgets and stunts were performed by the Lotus but the Aston Martin has become synonymous with James Bond. So much so that it was brought back in 1995 when Pierce Brosnan took over the roll and there was a Bond renaissance with *GoldenEye*. Simply put, the Aston Martin DB5 is James Bond's car.

The Aston Martin was first introduced in *Goldfinger* much like Bond was introduced in

The famous publicity photo of Sean Connery and the Aston Martin DB5 that helped catapult the car into infamy. This car, with British license plate BMT 216A, is the street-stock (no special effects) car used for "beauty" scenes in Goldfinger and Thunderball. All of the hydraulics and actuator motors that brought the gadgets to life on the stunt vehicle added over 300 pounds to the car. *Old Cars Weekly*

1964's *Goldfinger* made Aston Martin a household name. Not only was the Touring-designed DB5 aesthetically stunning, it was also a special-effects marvel filled with working secret weapons, including an ejector seat. *Everett Collection*

Dr. No. Early in the film Bond receives his assignment: learn Auric Goldfinger's secrets. Bond is told to report to "Q Branch," MI6's spy-gadget skunkworks. As the camera pans the facility, treating the viewer to far-fetched equipment tests, machine gun–proof outerwear, and poison gas parking meters, Bond asks Q for his Bentley. A very quotable exchange ensues:

Bond: "Where's my Bentley?"

Q: "It's had its day, I'm afraid."

Bond in dismay: "But it's never let me down."

Q: "M's orders. You'll be using this Aston Martin DB5 with modifications."

As the words leave his lips the frame is filled with a three-quarter front view of the silver car in the clean-room setting. Another legend was born.

The use of an Aston Martin "with modifications" was always intended for *Goldfinger,* but the specific model was not originally to be the DB5. In Fleming's 1959 novel of the same name, Bond was offered a choice of two company cars. He picked an Aston Martin DB MkIII over a Jaguar MkII because of its special features, and its styling better suited his cover as a swinging, well-heeled bachelor.

The special features included a secret compartment for a long-barreled Colt .45 under the driver seat, a receiver for the homing device hidden in the radio, steel front and rear bumpers for ramming or defense, and switches to change the color and configuration of the headlights and taillights to confuse anyone tailing him or the quarry he was following. Fleming never thought of left and right front wing machine guns, revolving number plates, and certainly not an ejector seat.

Those inventions were the brainchild of special effects guru John Stears, who worked on most of the Bond films, and production designer Ken Adam. Stears and Adam were instrumental in persuading Aston Martin to lend a DB5 for the film.

Initially the automaker was not interested in supplying the newly developed DB5 gratis and was bemused by the outrageous modifications the studio had in mind. Obviously the Aston Martin brass did not believe in the star-making potential of the film.

Stears would not settle for a substitute. He wanted to remain somewhat faithful to the original book, and the new DB5 was too fetching to pass up. After many pitches, Aston Martin agreed and loaned an early car to Stears and his team.

Aston versus Bentley

The choice of the DB5 was significant to the James Bond film franchise because the classic look and sex appeal of the car complemented the star and his occupation. It was the mechanical embodiment of Bond: suave and debonair with a cool exterior that belied the secrets it held inside. You simply cannot imagine Bond with any other vehicle; however, had Fleming not written the DB MkIII into *Goldfinger,* it is unlikely an Aston Martin would have been chosen for the films at all.

Fleming had a predilection for Bentleys, and throughout the novels Bond drove several different models, none with high-tech gadgetry beyond an Amherst Villiers supercharger. The three specific models Bond drove in the books were a 1930 4.5-liter convertible coupe, a 1953 Mark VI with an open touring body, and a 1954 Continental R. All were battleship gray and maintained by Bond himself, "his only personal hobby."

Bentleys do make cameo appearances in three films: *From Russia with Love* (1963), *Casino Royale* (1967), and *Never Say Never Again* (1983). All are 4.5-liter supercharged models, but each is black rather than the battleship gray specified by Fleming. The same color was specified for the DB MkIII in *Goldfinger,* but the car that became the star was originally Dubonnet Red.

Stears' and Adam's Car

Stears received chassis number DP-216-1 in January of 1963 and began transforming the car into Bond's ultimate rolling arsenal. The DP in the serial number stands for Development Project, which confirms this was the first DB5 ever built.

Stears had just six weeks to design and build a working car for the film, and like the character Q, Stears never joked about his work. The first order of business was to develop new and spectacular weapons worthy of the larger-than-life character.

Sean Connery poses on the passenger side of the Aston Martin DB5. This is the car used for the beauty shots. The stunt car had a hole cut in the roof on the passenger side, and an air cylinder under the seat fired a dummy through the roof for the climax of the chase scene in *Goldfinger. Photofest*

Some of Fleming's original ideas were incorporated, such as the homing device housed in the radio and the gun under the seat, but that is where the similarities ended and wild imagination took over.

All of the defensive mechanisms and weapons required a complex, 300-pound hydraulic system to operate. The special effects team routed tubing, cylinders, and pumps throughout the car with the main reservoirs and pump located in the trunk, so outwardly the car was unchanged. Amazingly, many of the devices were actually controlled from the center console as they were alleged to do in the film.

The bullet-deflecting steel plate that rose from the trunk lid was actually made of plastic. It raised and lowered on tracks under the trunk lid powered by a hydraulic motor. The sound effects added to the illusion that it was steel.

The triple taillight assemblies were consolidated onto one plane and rigged to swing downwards via a bowden cable operated from the doorsill on the driver-side floor. Once opened, a nitrogen-charged cylinder in the trunk sprayed colored water to simulate oil. The on-off switch was located in the console. The left-side taillight was similarly rigged but spewed four-spiked nails. This effect was not shown in the film.

The smoke screen Bond uses when fleeing Goldfinger's henchmen at his Swiss factory was simply a Brocks B4 smoke canister mounted

James Bond (Sean Connery) and Auric Goldfinger (Gert Frobe) look on as Oddjob (Harold Sakata) demonstrates his leathal headwear. The 1937 Rolls-Royce Phantom III Sedanca de Ville was seen through a major portion of *Goldfinger* and, in the story, was allegedly dismantled to smuggle gold. *Photofest*

under the rear of the car and set off at the time of filming.

Up front Stears created the illusion of Browning machine guns pushing forward from behind the turn-signal lights by hinging the lamp assembly at the bottom. Metal tubes were used to simulate gun barrels that moved forward and backward on a

gear system powered by electric motors, all of which were mounted inside the fenders. To get the lights to return to the closed position, a spring was connected to the barrel, so as it was retracted the lights moved back into position.

You may recall the guns actually fired during the chase sequences. The effect was achieved by feeding a mixture of oxygen and acetylene into the tubes. A spark plug mounted in the tubes and connected to the distributor ignited the gas mixture just as it would in the engine cylinder.

The revolving license plates, "valid in all countries, of course," were prominently demonstrated on screen and actually functioned via a lever in the console. The plates were mounted on a triangular frame with a central axis connected to a gear and spring. A miniature gearshift lever in the console could be moved to one of three positions for whichever plate was desired. A pin would lock the assembly in place after the next plate rolled over. The mechanism for the front plates was housed in a chrome-plated box attached to the bumper while the rear plates were mounted into the trunk lid. The three plate numbers were LU-67 89 (Switzerland), BMT 216A (England), and 4711-EA 62 (France).

The tracking system used to keep tabs on Goldfinger's 1937 Rolls-Royce Phantom III Sedan de Ville was hidden behind the radio speaker grille atop the transmission tunnel. Despite the high-tech sounds and appearance, it was actually a very low-tech effect. The grille was raised manually out of camera shot, and a stationary backlit map simulated Bond's radar system. The entire unit was completely fabricated and looked nothing like Aston Martin's standard radio unit. In fact, much of the unit was filmed outside of the car.

Stears' team went as far as simulating a radar scanner under the side view mirror, but it was never shown on film.

Other features that never made the big screen were the tray under the driver seat containing a pistol, hand grenade, and throwing knife, a telephone in the driver door, and the extending bumper overriders for ramming.

Steel tubes were connected to the individual overriders and passed through holes in the bumper. A hydraulic motor pushed the tubes forward. When the pressure was shut off from the console switch, a spring pulled them back into place.

The *Ben Hur*–like tire shredders used to derail Tilly Masterson's (Tania Mallet) Ford Mustang were quite ingenious. Had they been real it would have been an incredible accomplishment. The actual effect of the slashers extending from the hubs was done with a mock-up of the wheel and fender assembly of the car and a three-eared

knock-off welded to a steel tube. For the close-ups the tubes were simply pushed out through the hubs. The steel tubes were attached to the actual knock-offs for the long shots of the car with the slashers extended. Through careful editing it comes off very well.

The Most Famous Accessory

When it came time for Q to explain the most famous accessory, Bond's reply was equally memorable: an incredulous, "You're joking." It was no joke—it was real. The entire stunt was modeled after an actual aircraft ejector seat. It was set up to be done especially for the scene. Thankfully everything went as planned and it was caught on the first take.

A hole that opened when the actual seat was fired was cut into the roof panel. All of the interior scenes featured the normal car seat because the ejection seat was much larger. The stunt seat for the chase sequence was fitted at Auric Enterprises. A dummy was placed in the seat and a compressed air cylinder fired the seat-and-dummy package 15 feet into the air.

An actual Aston Martin gearshift lever was redesigned with a spring-loaded top and simple red button perched on a spring to look like the real McCoy.

Once Stears and his team had finished their work and reassembled the car, it was sent back to the factory to be painted. Silver Birch was chosen over Flemming's favorite battleship gray as more photogenic.

The car was ready for action at Pinewood Studios when filming commenced in March of 1964. A second Silver Birch DB5 was also brought in for the beauty shots and nonstunt sequences. If you are extremely sharp you can notice the subtle differences between the two cars.

Throughout the first half of the film we get to see most of the "modifications" in action, until the car gets destroyed at the culmination of the chase at Goldfinger's factory. As Bond said, "You'd be surprised about how much wear and tear goes on out there in the field."

The DB5 was reborn in the opening sequence of the next Bond film, *Thunderball*, in 1965. In the pretitle action Bond escapes the Chateau d'Anet palace via jetpack and lands next to his DB5. After neatly tucking the jetpack into the trunk, he raises the rear bulletproof screen and activates two water cannons mounted below the bumper to fend off the baddies firing upon him.

The water cannon trick was actually a very simple stunt. Two brackets were mounted under the rear bumper to hold actual fire hoses. A pumper fire truck was located off camera near the front of the car. On cue the water came full force to mow down the deadly gunman.

Later in the film we get another brilliant stunt sequence, but this time it involves a trick motorcycle that saves Bond and the Aston Martin. Count Lippe (Guy Doleman) in a black Ford Skyliner is pursuing Bond on a deserted stretch of highway. Bond goes for his defense mechanisms just as Lippe is about to close in for the kill, but Lippe is blown up by a rocket-shooting BSA 650 Lightning motorcycle.

Once again Stears and company masterminded the stunt. A trick fairing for the BSA featured two very pronounced chrome tubes protruding from each side of the bike. The rider was able to release Icarus military rockets through the tubes to simulate real rocket fire.

The convincing part of the stunt came when the back end of the Ford was blown up by the hail of rockets. Stears had rigged up the rear of the car with a fiberglass trunk lid and break-away body parts. Inside the trunk were 5 gallons of fuel and cordite that could be ignited on cue by the driver who sat inside the gutted interior. The driver door removed for a quick escape.

The entire sequence was filmed on a straight section of track at the Silverstone racing circuit made up to look like a country road. All three vehicles ran at an even speed and distance apart. At the predetermined moment the rockets were fired and the fuel was detonated. The trunk lid flew into the air, and the car was quickly engulfed in flames.

The thrilling stunt was capped off when the leather-clad motorcycle pilot dumped the bike off a cliff into the water. The helmet came off to reveal the sultry-but-deadly two-wheeled assassin Fiona Volpe, played by Luciana Paluzzi.

Just as Paluzzi did not do the actual riding, the BSA 650 was not thrown into the water. A stand-in BSA 10 was painted up to look like the rocket bike and used for the final sequence.

As Count Lippe's Ford is left to burn along the roadside, the rocket-bearing BSA shoots past

Bond, leaving us with the final frames of the Aston Martin DB5 on the big screen.

The Fate of the Original DB5

It would be some 30 years and 14 films later before we would see Bond behind the wheel of the DB5 again. When the series was reborn with Pierce Brosnan in the title role, the DB5 was a necessary link to the character as Brosnan brought elements of the Connery Bond forward in his 1995 debut, GoldenEye. This time, however, the car does not perform stunts or show any of its unique arsenal. Instead we are treated to a stirring game of cat-and-mouse as Bond in the DB5 and Xenia Onatop (Famke Janssen) in a Ferrari 355 GTS roar through the winding mountain roads that lead to Monaco.

From that point on the DB5 has made appearances in each of the Brosnan Bond films as Bond's personal car.

The actual DB5 built by Stears for Goldfinger and Thunderball is currently owned by a private collector in Boca Raton, Florida. The story of how it got there is as good as any Bond movie script.

After two years on tour to promote the films, the car was returned to Aston Martin because it was originally on loan to the studios. Rather than preserve this piece of history, the Aston Martin company committed the ultimate crime by stripping all the high-tech gadgetry and returning it to a road-going car. It remained at the factory until 1969, when it was purchased by a private party with the full documentation of what the car once was, even though the commission number was changed.

After the owner had seen a lot of press and escalating prices for the beauty car used in the films and a promotional car that was built by the studios, he hired a restoration shop to re-install the mock weapons. Although they were not completely faithful reproductions, it all worked and he had the certificates to prove the authenticity of the car. It was later sold and moved to Florida.

The beauty car is also in private hands in the United States while the studio promotional car is on display in the Smoky Mountain Car Museum in Tennessee. The original gadget car has not made a public appearance since the New York Auto Show in 1981. It was in the news briefly in 1997 when it was stolen from a locked hangar at the Boca Raton airport. The car was quickly recovered and returned to the rightful owner.

The first time we witness the real power behind the arsenal of modifications in the Aston Martin DB5 is when Bond uses the tire shredders housed in the knock-off hubs to disable the 1965 Ford Mustang convertible. *Old Cars Weekly*

Toyota built two 2000 GT convertibles expressly for use in the 1967 release *You Only Live Twice.* The car did not feature any secret weapons such as machine guns or oil slicks. Instead it featured many electronic gadgets including a closed-circuit TV and video phone. Toyota was disappointed the movie did not bring them as much notoriety as Aston Martin received in earlier Bond films. *Everett Collection*

CHAPTER 2

James Bond: Beyond British

In Connery's next caper, 1967's *You Only Live Twice,* Bond, who is undercover in Japan, introduces us to an exciting new one-of-a-kind vehicle. This time, however, it is not Bond's car.

This story has Bond on assignment in Tokyo to thwart SPECTRE's plan to start a war among the world superpowers by stealing American and Russian manned spaceships. A very ambitious plot and some good special effects, especially the secret volcano lair of SPECTRE's rocket base.

The kicker to this film is the opening pre-credit sequence showing our hero getting ambushed and killed. Or so we are led to believe.

There is a fair amount of time spent showing Japanese culture as Bond gets help from M's opposite number, Tiger Tanaka (Tetsuro Tamba), and Japanese agent Aki (Akiko Wakabayashi).

Bond Turns Japanese

The lovely Aki drives a white Toyota 2000 GT convertible with several optional extras that M fondly calls modifications. Besides the car itself, the most interesting feature of the car is that it is a convertible.

Toyota shocked the world when it introduced the 2000 GT at the Tokyo Motor Show in 1965. It was a sleek, sexy sports car well ahead of its time by Japanese automobile standards, looking more like it came from the pen of an Italian design studio. A double overhead cam, two-liter, six-cylinder engine that pumped out 150 horsepower with the aid of three sidedraft Solex carburetors resided under the hood. Unfortunately it proved to be too far ahead of its time, and production ceased in 1967 after just 337 cars were produced. Two cars that were not part of the published production numbers were customized and used for the 1967 Bond film.

Toyota offered to build a very special car to use in the film and customized two units from the windshield pillars back. The entire rear of the car had to be restructured to make it rigid enough as a convertible. The rear valance and taillight assemblies were retained from the original car.

Once completed the cars were turned over to John Stears to load them with the latest gadgetry. This time the goodies were electronic communication gizmos, including a miniature color television, closed-circuit television with forward- and rear-facing cameras hidden behind the license plates, wireless telephone, and a video recorder in the glovebox.

Despite all of the work that went into the car, only the closed-circuit television, wireless phone, and color TV are shown in one chase scene from the film.

Similarly, all the work Toyota put into the convertible version of the car did not bring the instant fame that Aston Martin enjoyed after *Goldfinger.* Production of the 2000 GTs was short lived and the only two convertible versions ever built were for the film. One of the cars remains in the Toyota museum.

After five films Connery became concerned about being type-cast for repeatedly playing Bond, so in 1969 ex-model George Lazenby tried on the Bond mantle for *On Her Majesty's Secret Service.*

This is one of the more forgettable Bond films simply because it was not Sean Connery in the lead. The story was a little more down to earth compared to the previous films, and Lazenby was an unknown quantity.

American Motors Corporation sponsored 1974's *Man with the Golden Gun* as AMC cars appeared throughout the film. In this scene, an AMC Hornet coupe barrel-rolls over the Thai River. This was a highly technical stunt designed with the aid of an aeronautical computer to take into account the car's speed and weight. *Photofest*

This time Bond battles Blofeld's plan to wage germ warfare from a converted Swiss allergy clinic. There are a few good chases on skis and bobsleds but Telly Savalas was not terribly menacing as Blofeld, and there was too much of Lazenby in a kilt and frilly shirts. The subplot has Bond falling in love and uncharacteristically getting married at the close of the film. Unfortunately, the marriage was very brief.

At the end of the film, Bond and new bride, Tracy (Diana Rigg), are ambushed by Blofeld, and she is killed by a hailstorm of bullets. Tracy died because the Aston Martin DBS they were riding in turned out to be an everyday car and had none of Q's modifications, which usually included bullet-proof glass and armor plating.

Throughout the film, Bond's DBS does not see very much action. Actually it's Tracy's 1969 orange Mercury Cougar convertible that gets driven harder and does more tire squealing (on snow) than any other vehicle. It is a bit inexplicable

what a brand-new American convertible is doing in the Swiss Alps in the wintertime, especially when it appears at the opening of the film on a beach in Portugal.

Detroit Does Bond

Lazenby quit after one film, and Connery was persuaded to renew his license to kill in 1971 with the release of *Diamonds Are Forever*. This was more of a typical Bond caper as he defeats Blofeld (Charles Gray) and SPECTRE's plans for world domination from the Las Vegas strip.

In this film Blofeld sets up shop in the penthouse of the Whyte House (actually the Las Vegas Hilton). The hotel is supposed to be owned by a reclusive multimillionaire (Jimmy Dean) named Willard Whyte, who is patterned after Howard Hughes.

Blofeld is holding the world ransom with control of a laser satellite powered by a refractive solar shield made of diamonds. Bond and femme

So that's a Matador?! In one of the more farcical moments in James Bond history, a 1974 AMC Matador was fitted with wings and a fake jet engine that allowed the villian to escape. The car did not actually fly, and the flying scenes were done with a model. *Patrick Foster*

fatale Tiffany Case (Jill St. John) defeat Blofeld, and two assassins of questionable sexuality to save the world.

Unfortunately Connery did not bring his car back with him; there is but one shot of his Aston Martin DB5 in Q's shop near the beginning of the film. The rest of the cars in the film were all sponsored by Ford Motor Company.

It was quite remarkable how all the cars on the streets and in parking lots were new-for-1971 Ford products. The only noteworthy car was the red Mustang Mach 1 that Bond and Tiffany Case use to elude the Las Vegas police.

After a comical chase through a parking lot, Bond stands the Mustang up on two wheels to negotiate a narrow alley. If you were paying attention

you would also notice one of the biggest gaffs in Bond film history as the car goes into the alley on the right wheels and comes out on the left wheels.

Bond on a Bike

After 1971, Connery finally had his fill and hung up his Walther PPK for good, or so he said.

In 1983, Connery came back as Bond in *Never Say Never Again*. This film was not an EON production; rather, it was a modernized makeover of *Thunderball*. The story was average but Klaus Maria Brandauer was sufficiently evil as Largo, and Connery clearly had a good time making light of his previous films.

True to the Bond book origins we get a glimpse of the Bentley as Connery drives up to a spa. Alas it is only a brief glimpse. Later in the film there is a short but notable sequence in which Bond climbs aboard a trick Yamaha XJ650 Turbo to chase Fatima Blush (Barbara Carrera) in her Renualt R5 Turbo.

The radically faired bike fired rockets, had a shield that dropped down behind the rear wheel to prevent the bike from being rammed, and was equipped with a rocket booster that helped Bond escape his captors by flying over them. Despite all these capabilities, Bond inexplicably crashes the bike in the tight quarters of a warehouse shortly after going airborne.

The bike and its gadgets were built by the Warner Bros. studio and the riding stunts performed by Mike Runyard. The location of the motorcycle is unknown.

The James Bond reins were handed to Roger Moore in 1973 for the eighth film in the series, *Live and Let Die*. Through the following 12 years, Moore returned to the big screen eight times to save the world from evil-doers and put his own brand on the Bond mantle.

The Bond that Moore crafted had a softer edge than his predecessor, but the stories and stunts had become bigger, wilder, and as far-fetched as the imagination could take you. Take, for example, an assassin named Jaws (Richard Kiel, introduced in 1977's *The Spy Who Loved Me*) who murders his quarry with his razor-sharp, stainless-steel teeth. Moore played all the films as they were designed—with a smirk on his face and his tongue firmly planted in his cheek.

It was not until his third film, *Spy*, that Moore finally got his signature car, the 1977 Lotus Esprit. The car made quite a splash in its debut with a couple of big stunts that permanently identified it as Roger Moore's Bond car. Surprisingly it was only actually used in two of Moore's eight films, and it did little in its second appearance but self-destruct.

The rest of the Moore era offered little in the way of cars, though there were a handful of stunts and vehicles worthy of mention.

Starting back at the beginning, the bizarre voodoo drug smuggler story line in *Live and Let Die* never had the chance to offer any vehicles (or make sense, for that matter) beyond some New York City taxicabs and an ostentatious Cadillac "pimpmobile" that simply hurt to look at.

Buzzing Hornets, Flying Matadors, and Half-Baked Alliances

In 1974, Moore returned to hunt down super-assassin Francisco Scaramanga (Christopher Lee) in a kill-or-be-killed dirge called *The Man with the Golden Gun* that was short on action and long on dialogue. It must be noted that the vehicles that appeared in the film were all sponsored by American Motors Corporation. This sponsorship is the only way to explain Bond driving a Hornet.

Bond steals the red Hornet about midway through the film from an AMC showroom in downtown Bangkok to chase Scaramanga's fleeing bronze-colored Matador. The mere mention of those two models of cars in pursuit of one another hardly puts you on the edge of your seat. In order to add some pep to the chase, the bumbling redneck Louisiana Sheriff J. W. Pepper (Clifton James) happens to be sitting in the car Bond steals while Bond's lovely-but-dopey co-agent (Britt Ekland) is locked in the trunk of the Matador.

During the chase sequence the Hornet performs a 360-degree barrel role in the process of jumping the Thai River on the remnants of a collapsed bridge. This was a highly technical, well-crafted stunt designed specifically to spin the car on its axis in midair. The entire sequence was choreographed with the aid of an aeronautical computer that specified vehicle speed, weight, distance, and trajectory. Pieces of the bridge remnants were strategically absent to make the car rotate at a specific speed and then catch the car as it completed the spin. Unfortunately the effect was diminished by the use of a slide whistle.

The chase ends at the limits of absurdity as Scaramanga escapes by driving inside a bamboo hangar where he clamps wings and a jet engine to the Matador and flies to his island hideaway. The flying Matador scenes were all obviously done with a model, while the dashboard transformation of auto gauges to avionics was done with a mocked-up dashboard outside of the car.

Fast forward to 1981's *For Your Eyes Only* as Bond and Melina (Carole Bouquet) demolish a Citroen 2CV while careening down a mountainside. The ridiculously titled *Octopussy* of 1983 offers only some high-speed driving in an Alfa Romeo GTV stolen by Bond. *A View to a Kill* in 1985 was Moore's last Bond epic, and his last car

When Roger Moore replaced Sean Connery as James Bond, a 1977 Lotus Esprit replaced the Aston Martin as the gadget car. In *The Spy Who Loved Me,* the Lotus converted to a submarine after being chased from a pier. An actual one-man submarine was made from a Lotus body shell.

The Lotus submersible was made from a Lotus Esprit body shell by Perry Submarine Company of Florida. The "car" was propelled by electric motors mounted on the rear bumper. A driver, disguised by the louvers, sat inside wearing scuba gear and piloted the car for the underwater scenes.

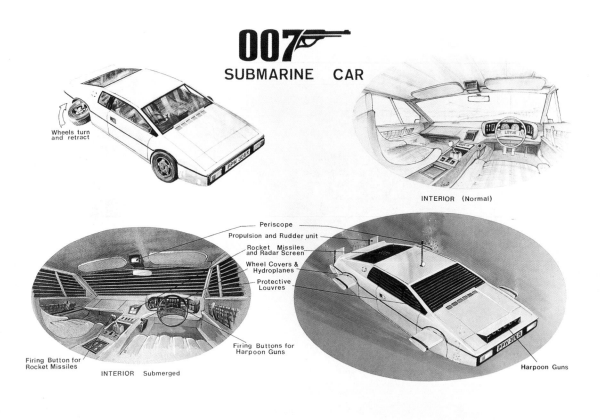

007 SUBMARINE CAR

Wheels turn and retract

INTERIOR (Normal)

Periscope
Propulsion and Rudder unit
Rocket Missiles and Radar Screen
Wheel Covers & Hydroplanes
Protective Louvres

Firing Button for Rocket Missiles

INTERIOR Submerged

Firing Buttons for Harpoon Guns

Harpoon Guns

The blueprints showing how the Lotus converted to a submarine and detailing the location of the weapons at Bond's disposal. *Photofest*

stunt was the inauspicious, far-fetched pursuit sequence through the streets of Paris driving the front half of a Renault Alliance after a series of Three Stooges–inspired crashes.

Roger Moore Gets a Real Bond Car

The best car—and the best story—in Moore's tenure was 1977's *The Spy Who Loved Me.* The film, costarring Barbara Bach as Soviet agent Triple-X, is widely acclaimed as Moore's best effort in the title role and where he finally gets a Bondian gadget car.

In this episode Bond is tracking the disappearance of American, British, and Russian nuclear submarines. In the process he comes up against Soviet Major Anya Amasova (Bach), and the two join forces to thwart the web-fingered recluse Karl Stromberg (Curt Jurgens), whose plan is to destroy terrestrial life in favor of undersea living.

The use of the white Lotus Esprit came about through the mutual admiration of Bond series pro-

ducer Cubby Broccoli and Lotus PR man Don McLaughlin. Broccoli was fond of the Georgio Giugiaro–penned styling while McLaughlin was keen to get the car into a Bond film, hoping for the same notoriety achieved by Aston Martin. A chance meeting of the two men put the car into the film.

The car, known as "Wet Nellie" to MI6, comes into the film unannounced and without the customary tour of its tricks by Q in his laboratory. Instead we suddenly find the car in Bond's possession in Sardinia while he is spying on the bad guys.

The car finally struts its stuff when 007 and Triple-X are pursued by the bodacious villianess Naomi (Caroline Munro) piloting Stromberg's killer helicopter. Just when it looks like the car and its occupants are trapped, the Lotus roars down a pier, plunging nose-first into the Mediterranean Sea.

As the audience sat with mouths agape, an underwater camera revealed the car transforming

A Lotus dummy car was used in this scene to depict the submarine car driving out of the water. The stunt was performed by using hidden tracks, cable, and winch. *Photofest*

James Bond was relaunched in 1995's *GoldenEye* after a six-year hiatus. The new Bond was a throwback to the original character created by Sean Connery. To help achieve that transformation, the Silver Birch Aston Martin DB5 was brought back as Bond's personal car. Pierce Brosnan poses with the car. *Aston Martin*

BMW participated in a media blitz to launch the new Bond film in 1995 and to promote Bond's newest car: the BMW Z3. The monsterous advertising budget created great anticipation. However, the car had only a brief screen appearance, and gadgetry was only hinted at. Here Pierce Brosnan and Isabella Scorupco pose with the Z3 during its cameo. *BMW*

itself into a submarine. The wheels retracted into the bodywork and were replaced with flush-fitting panels, a periscope rose from the roof, louvers covered the windows, dashboard instruments flipped over, and a bank of four propellers and steering gear extended from the rear bumper.

This effect was all done with a series of Lotus Esprit cars and body shells. To create the illusion of flying off the pier into the water, a Lotus shell with wheels propelled by a CO_2 tank was shot down the jetty with dummies on board.

The Perry Submarine Company in Florida created the phenomenal underwater Lotus Esprit. One Esprit shell was used to simulate the transformation from car to sub, while an actual submersible was made from a second Lotus body shell. The Lotus

submarine was propelled by four electric motors at the back of the car. A "driver" sat inside the unit in full scuba gear, his presence disguised by the louvers covering all of the glass. At one point there was a plan to prevent the driver's exhale bubbles from escaping out of the car to make it more like a real submarine. To achieve this the driver would have to use a rebreather, but the idea was scrapped in the name of safety.

The real Lotus submersible was capable of diving to 300 feet and carried a two-hour supply of air in its tanks. The sub driver also actuated the various defense mechanisms from inside the car, such as the Limpet mines, torpedoes, and smoke screens. Small servo motors opened small panels in the bodywork to simulate the defense

An example of one of the great verbal sparring scenes between Q (Desmond Llewelyn) and Bond (Pierce Brosnan) as Bond takes possession of the BMW 750iL in *Tomorrow Never Dies*. *Everett Collection*

systems. The surface-to-air missiles that brought down Naomi's helicopter were done with an underwater model and a model helicopter.

To achieve the underwater scene where Bond and Amasova observe the undersea legs of "Atlantis," Stromberg's floating hideout, a radio-controlled model Lotus motored past the simulated structure.

The Lotus' final scene as a submarine—in which our heroes drive out of the sea onto a crowded beach—was done by laying tracks into the water and pulling a dummy car up the tracks with a winch. The tracks and cable were strategically hidden by the sand. Naturally the campy scene was played to the hilt as in all Moore films.

Most of the outdoor or underwater sequences were filmed by a location crew in the Bahamas. Meanwhile Moore and Bach did all of their filming in a pool at the Pinewood Studios in London.

No series of films has launched as many memorable cars and car stunts as the franchise of James Bond films. Collectively, all of the cars and

films in this book cannot hold a candle to the 20 blockbuster movies featuring Bond's gadget-laden spy cars and the thrilling pursuit sequences that are integral to each story line.

When the smoke clears, and there was always smoke, three marques are instantly identified with Bond: Aston Martin, Lotus, and BMW.

Bond Buys a Beemer

By the late 1980s it appeared audiences suffered from a bit of Bond-burnout. Perhaps the end of the Cold War eliminated the need for international espionage, or perhaps star wars were more interesting than spy wars. Nonetheless, Dalton had done a credible job in the role but ticket sales were lackluster by previous standards, so Bond went on hiatus for six years.

In 1995, Pierce Brosnan was fitted for the Bond tuxedo in *GoldenEye*. Brosnan played it closer to the Connery style with the propensity to use the license to kill rather than Moore's license to quip.

BMW's unabashed sponsorship of the 1990s Bond came to the forefront in 1997's *Tomorrow Never Dies.* **The BMW 750iL was driven by remote control from the back seat. Gadgets included missiles that fired from the moonroof, the ability to drive on flat tires, armour plating, and a safe in the glovebox.** *BMW*

To help ensure the link to Connery's Bond, a 1965 Silver Birch Aston Martin DB5 was brought back as Bond's personal car. It was not, however, THE Aston with THE modifications; even the license plate was two digits off of Connery's car. Instead it was a regular street version of the car, but its appearance in the film was far from pedestrian.

As Bond is being analyzed by an MI6 psychologist during a drive through the south of France, he is suddenly challenged on the road by a 1995 Ferrari 355 GTS. Not one to back down, Bond dices with the Ferrari on the twisting roads leading to Monte Carlo. Great camera work and solid stunt driving make the sequence a real treat for the audience.

The appearance of the Aston Martin was a complete surprise because the car that garnered

all the pre-premiere buzz was the BMW Z3. The Bavarian auto manufacturer had "bought" themselves the Bond car as a pre-release publicity stunt and it worked. The sexy-looking-but-underpowered new two-seater was highly publicized as the new Bond car in every ad and every trailer. Unfortunately its appearance in the film was a major letdown.

We first see the Atlanta-Blue BMW when Bond reports to Q's workshop after being assigned to stop some renegade Russians and their stolen controls for satellite weapons. In this sequence we see a parachute deploy from the rear of the car, and we think we are in for some real thrills with this new ride.

The car's next appearance is late in the film as Bond and heroine Izabella Scorupco drive through a plantation in Cuba before Bond tosses

One of the spectacular pyrotechnic stunts characteristic of Bond films as the 750iL survives a rocket attack. *BMW*

A crashing end for the 750iL in *Tomorrow Never Dies. BMW*

The BMW R1200 cruiser made a big splash as a getaway vehicle for Pierce Brosnan and Michelle Yeoh in Bangkok, Thailand. The motorcycle had no gadgets but performed many exciting stunts including this building-to-building jump. *BMW*

the keys to CIA man Jack Wade (Joe Don Baker). In total the car is on screen for four minutes and does not perform one stunt nor even drive quickly. It was all sizzle and no steak and a total letdown for all Bond gadget-lovers.

When Bond tossed the keys to Wade he eluded to the possible gadgets, but they were never seen.

Bond: "Just one thing, don't push any of the buttons in that car."

Wade: "I'm just going to go bombing around in it."

Bond: "Exactly!"

BMW and EON Productions partnered to make the new roadster Bond's official car. Rather than paying a license, BMW agreed to prominently promote the new film with its ads for the Z3, and it had 20 cars on hand for the U.S. premiere.

Unfortunately for BMW, film production ran well ahead of auto production, so two hand-built cars were made for use in the film.

Whether or not the car did any stunts is beside the point. The real news was that a British agent drove a German car. Everyone knows that creator Ian Fleming would never have put Bond in anything but an English-built car. One could make the argument that BMW had British ties after buying Rover, but it is still a stretch.

The success of the partnership brought both parties back to the table for the next Bond installment, 1997's *Tomorrow Never Dies*. This saga sends Bond to Hamburg to investigate the megalomaniac Elliot Carver (Jonathan Pryce), who is secretly staging international catastrophes so he can control the world's media. Certainly an interesting

BMW's sexy new Z8 debuted on screen in 1999 in *The World Is Not Enough.* The five-liter, 400-horsepower beauty had a very short life in the film before being chopped in half. Because the car was so new, there was no time to install actual props into the car. The stunts were done in close-up, so they only had to show mock-ups of the car fenders and steering wheel. *BMW*

twist on world domination, and he has some very unique methods for obtaining his goals.

In order to defeat and escape, Carver and his henchmen Bond utilize both two-wheeled and four-wheeled BMWs. However, rather than retrieving them from MI6 headquarters he "rents" a BMW 750iL at the Hamburg airport from Q posing as a rental car agent. The quips between the two men as they go through the typical rental car rhetoric is a priceless Bond-Q exchange.

Q: "If you'll just sign here, Mr. Bond. It's the insurance damage waiver for your beautiful new car. Will you need collision coverage?"

Bond: "Yes."

Q: "Fire?"

Bond: "Probably."

Q: "Property destruction?"

Bond: "Definitely."

Q: "Personal injury?"

Bond: "I hope not, but accidents do happen."

Q: "They frequently do with you."

Bond: "Well, that takes care of the normal wear and tear. Do I need any other protection?"

Q: "Only from me, 007, unless you bring that car back in pristine order."

As it turns out, this Q-ship is one of Bond's most technologically advanced weapons ever. Naturally the body and glass are both fireproof and bulletproof. The exterior of the car is also electrified to deliver an immobilizing jolt to would-be thieves. All four tires are re-inflatable using a rubber solution that is sprayed outward from the center of the wheel and inflated with small compressed air canisters mounted on the center hub.

Inside the car the glovebox contains a safe and spare pistol—a Walther PPK, of course. The glovebox can only be opened via fingerprint ID programmed to only recognize 007.

The metal sunroof actually hides 12 heat-seeking missiles, tire-puncturing spikes spray from beneath the rear bumper, and the blue-and-white roundel on the hood houses a motorized, metal-eating cutter.

To top it all off, Bond is able to drive the car by remote control with a secret pad and video monitor hidden in his trick cell phone. "Let's see how she responds to my touch," he says as he promptly spins the car around and then brings it to a halt inches from Q via remote control. Hoping to appeal to Bond's senses, Q also engineered a breathy female

voice into the car's safety system. (If the BMW marketing angle of the film was overt, then the Ericsson cell phone plug was totally over the top.)

While this was to have been one of the most advanced Bond cars ever, little was actually done to a 750iL in comparison to the original DB5. Most all of the tricks the car performed were the high-speed driving stunts with a driverless car in a parking garage before it crashed through the barriers and plunged into a storefront window along the street below.

The parking ramp sequence was as exciting as any chase in a Bond film, but aside from Bond driving the car while lying in the back seat, the gadgets were done in close-up to disguise the fact that the car was not retooled.

In another bit of superb vehicular choreography, Bond and Chinese agent Wai Lin (Michelle

Yeoh) escaped Carver's men aboard a new BMW R1200 motorcycle. The bike had no defensive weapons or special performance features, but it was ridden brilliantly through the streets of Saigon and even eluded a helicopter.

Bond returned to action in *The World Is Not Enough,* debuting in the fall of 1999. This one is as action-packed as a Bond film could be. Bond chases a madman bent on destroying the Western powers and a deceitful beauty with personal ties to M (Judi Dench) from the mountaintops of Azerbaijan to a deserted castle in the Istanbul harbor.

The Aston Martin DB5 again makes a brief appearance as Bond's personal car when he pulls up to the "office" at MI6 headquarters near the opening of the film, but Bond's stylish-but-deadly field car again bares the BMW emblem. This

A Z8 was transported to Azerbaijan and hung full of cameras to show Bond (Pierce Brosnan) in action with the car. These scenes did not make the final editor's cut and were not seen in the movie. On a side note, this was Q's final appearance as the master gadget maker. In the story, Q retires. Coincidentally and sadly, Desmond Llewelyn died in a traffic accident shortly after *The World Is Not Enough* was released. *BMW*

time it is the stunning 1999 Z8 roadster, but like its slower cousin, the Z3, it unfortunately has only a brief cameo appearance in the film.

Mostly the Z8 sits and looks handsome in the misty night air at the caviar docks of Bond's Russian friend Valentin Zukovsky (Robbie Coltrane). When the men are attacked by helicopters dangling wild buzz-saw contraptions, Bond engages the BMW's concealed Stinger missiles. The car carries two missiles, one on each side hidden behind the vents in the front fenders. The LED targeting system

operates through the BMW logo in the center of the steering wheel. Unfortunately Bond is only able to destroy one of the two helicopters before the second comes along and cuts the car in half longitudinally.

The LED steering wheel and missile-deploying side vents were all shot close-up, indicating that a real Z8 was not modified for the film. The fender sections and steering wheel were fabricated specifically for these stunts. In fact, an actual Z8 was barely off the assembly line and available for the filming.

Nicolas Cage poses alongside the modern-day Eleanor, a 1967 Shelby Mustang GT 500. A dummy car was used for the final chase sequence. *Photofest*

CHAPTER 3

Cops and Robbers

Forget suspense, plots, and character development—when it comes down to the memorable films in this book, we are talking chase scenes. Many, many films have had chase scenes, some humorous like the Keystone Cops, some short but thrilling as in 1971's *The French Connection*, and finally those that can make or break the film as in 1998's Ronin.

These are the scenes that keep you coming back time and time again, comparing notes with friends and even memorizing counts on your VCR so you know right where to begin watching.

The chase scene in *Bullitt* was groundbreaking because it was done on city streets and filmed at full speed. It featured incredible high-speed action that put you inside the various cars used in the scene and opened the door for a huge number of films that followed.

When *Gone in 60 Seconds* bowed in theaters in 1974, Toby Halicki proved a chase scene can be very long and very entertaining. In 1978's *Smokey and the Bandit*, Burt Reynolds took it one step further, crafting an entire film around a chase scene.

Bullitt (1968)

Warner Bros.
Director: Peter Yates
Starring: Steve McQueen and Robert Vaughn, Jacqueline Bisset, Robert Duvall

Bullitt made movie history when it debuted in 1968, but its historic significance had nothing to do with the screenplay, the cinematography, or the acting. It was the 10 minutes of footage featuring a 1968 Ford Mustang 390 GT squaring off against a 1968 Dodge Charger 440 Magnum that catapulted this movie to immortality.

The chase scene is what put *Bullitt* on the must-see list in 1968 and what keeps it on the must-see list today. It was the first chase scene filmed in real-time with real sound on real streets. And not just any streets: these were the mighty inclines of San Francisco, California.

The story line is almost unimportant. In fact, if you have the movie on tape you have no doubt watched the chase scene more than the full story, but in case you forgot, here's how it goes: Steve McQueen is a hard-nosed cop assigned to protect a mobster who is about to testify against his former employers. When his charge is killed, McQueen goes after the bad guys, but the bad guys know he knows who they are so they want to get him first. Got it?

McQueen drives a dark-green 1968 Mustang GT fastback with a 390-ci engine and a four-speed transmission. The car was chosen because it looked like a car a cop would drive in 1968.

The hitmen drive a jet-black 1968 Dodge Charger powered by a 440 Magnum and a four-speed transmission. The Dodge was chosen because the team working on the picture felt there were too many Fords already being used in the film.

The studio purchased two identical Mustangs and two identical Chargers. The Mustangs were bought through a promotional program Ford had with the studio, but the Dodges were bought off a lot in Glendale, California, because Chrysler did not have a budget with Warner Bros. at the time.

Top Hollywood wrench Max Balchowski prepped the cars for the grueling stunts and action scenes. The Mustangs received reinforced shock towers, new cross-members, stiffer springs, and Koni shocks. All suspension parts were magnafluxed for improved durability. TorqueThrust wheels and oversized tires were also mounted on the car.

Under the hood the heads were milled and aftermarket ignition and headers were installed.

Far less was done to the Dodge. All suspension parts were again magnafluxed, and flat springs were welded in the rear to keep the back end from jacking up. The front end got stronger torsion bars and control arms along with heavy-duty shocks. Nothing was done to the motor.

When it came to the actual filming, the chase scene was made up on the spot. They would rehearse the scenes at half speed and then film at full speed. Logistically it was difficult be-cause the film crew could only close a handful of streets at a time and only had two police officers assigned to handle the traffic.

Cars were parked strategically along the route to protect personal property and add realism. That worked well, but you can spot the same VW Beetle several times during the chase.

There is a lot of debate as to how much of the actual driving McQueen did. According to a 1987 article in *Musclecar Review*, McQueen certainly intended to do all the stunt driving. However, during rehearsal he overcooked a few corners and was replaced by a stunt driver.

One way to tell if McQueen is driving on the in-car footage is to look at the rearview mirror: If you can see McQueen he is obviously the driver; otherwise the mirror is tipped so you cannot see the driver's face. Most of the Mustang scenes were done by stunt driver Bud Ekins.

Max Balchowski, Hollywood's top wrench, prepped two identical 1968 Mustangs for the chase sequences on the hilly streets of San Francisco. Modifications included reinforced shock towers. Stiffer springs, Koni shocks, and all suspension parts were magnafluxed for extra durability. *Randy Leffingwell*

There have been many searches and false claims, but neither of the Mustangs used in the film survive today. People close to the film substantiate that both cars were sold to Warner Brothers employees after the filming, but the cars have never resurfaced. This faithful reproduction, right down to the TorqueThrust wheels, was built by David Kunz and can be viewed in detail at http://people.freenet.de/pony/bullitj.htm. *Randy Leffingwell*

The "actor" who played the driver of the Charger was in fact top Hollywood stunt driver Bill Hickman. It just so happened that Hickman's looks fit the part, and since it was a nonspeaking role it worked out nicely.

During the action sequences the cars took a horrible beating and began falling apart. The cars topped 100 miles per hour in order to catch as much air as they did. To capture the tremendous impact of the landings, a camera was hard-mounted into the back of each car.

The Charger lost countless hubcaps during the chase, and when the cars started ramming each other many more parts fell off of both vehicles.

The final sequence takes place on Guadalupe Canyon Highway south of San Fran. McQueen's Mustang was rigged with a towing mechanism that allowed the Charger to be towed alongside the Ford. At the right moment stunt driver Ekins released the Charger, which carried two dummies, sending the Charger careening into a gas station that was rigged to explode. The car actually missed the station but the charges went off and the scene still worked.

Despite all this heart-pounding action, the best scene may be at the beginning of the chase when the hitman looks in his rearview mirror and McQueen's Mustang swings into view.

As the movie achieved cult status, a lot was made about the fate of the cars used in the movie. Many have tried to track them down, including McQueen himself.

Obviously one of the Chargers was destroyed in the climax of the chase. The second Charger seems to have simply faded into history.

The *Bullitt* chase scene was revolutionary because it was filmed at real speed on city streets. It also had a camera inside the car for a driver's-eye view of the action during those torrid jumps. McQueen's prowess behind the wheel is well documented, however he only did 50 percent of the driving for the chase sequence. When McQueen is actually at the wheel, you can see him in the rearview mirror. When the stunt driver is at the wheel, the mirror is tilted away. Originally McQueen had planned to do all of the driving, but during practice he over-cooked a corner and the director chose to have stunt driver Bud Ekins sit in. *Randy Leffingwell*

As for the Mustangs, both were believed to be sold to Warner Bros. studio employees, one a secretary and the other a messenger. Bud Ekins substantiates one of the stories because they had to rent the car back from the secretary to re-record some sounds that were not picked up during the chase.

Since then the cars have likely been sold to second-, third-, and fourth-party owners. No one has substantiated the existence of either car to this day.

The Italian Job (1969)

Oakhurst Productions/Paramount Pictures
Director: Peter Collinson
Starring: Michael Caine, Noel Coward, Benny Hill, Raf Vallone, Rossano Brazzi, and Margaret Blye

The Italian Job is a film approaching cult-classic status for car lovers. Albeit very dated, this comedy-caper is a vintage sports car thrill-ride featuring an automotive cast that rivals any Cecil B. De Mille epic:

Lamborghini, Jaguar, Aston Martin, Austin Mini, and a throng of Fiats and Alfa Romeos.

The opener is a real grabber. Serene music plays as you watch a bright orange Lamborghini Muira speeding gracefully through the Alps driven by a cigarette smoking Mafioso-type who suddenly meets his demise by running head-on into a bulldozer.

It is a great opening sequence because you are drawn in by the seductive shape of the Muira at speed and then put on the edge of your seat because the car is destroyed and pushed off a cliff.

The story itself is the underdog-winning-against-impossible-odds cliché; forget the fact that they are all crooks. Michael Caine stars as Charlie Croker, a groovy 1960s hipster and two-bit thief. Caine's performance is so campy you would think you were watching Austin Powers thirty years before Mike Meyers invented the character.

Cars took center stage and billing in this poster for *The Italian Job.*

Our "hero" inherits a plan from his boss, the former Lamborghini driver, to steal $4 million in gold bullion from Italian auto manufacturer Fiat.

The plan is to boost the gold as it is being transported through Turin during the England versus Italy soccer match, load the bars into three Mini Coopers, and escape while the city is paralyzed in a massive traffic jam.

In order to pull it off, Charlie needs the backing of the U.K.'s biggest crime boss, Mr. Bridger, played by Noel Coward in his last screen performance.

With Bridger's support, Charlie hires a group of rally drivers to pilot the three getaway Mini Coopers. They rehearse the getaway in a warehouse, destroying several cars in the process. Unfortunately, the real Mafia gets wind of their plan.

On the way to Italy, Charlie and the gang encounter that same menacing bulldozer, which wreaks havoc with Charlie's Aston Martin DB4 convertible, Series 1 Jaguar E-Type coupe, and Series 1 E-Type roadster.

Charlie's gang eventually pulls off the heist with the help of an eccentric computer genius played by Benny Hill. His character, Simon Peach, sabotages the city traffic computers before falling victim to his infatuation for large women.

The ensuing chase scenes are a bit cartoonish but feature some outstanding stunt driving as the Minis elude thousands of Fiats and Alfas. The three Minis drive through sewers, the subway, and a wedding before making an incredible rooftop-to-rooftop jump. This jump was filmed on the roof of the Fiat factory. Some crew members walked off for fear it would end in a fatality, and the Italian Fiat workers made the sign of the cross to the stuntmen. The cars actually performed the jump, which required speeds in excess

Michael Caine and an Aston Martin DB5 convertible enroute to steal the payroll of the Fiat Motor Company. Caine, as Charlie Croker, puts on airs with the use of exotic cars such as this Aston and a Jaguar E-Type coupe. These two cars along with a Lamborghini Muira are destroyed in the film. *Photofest*

of 50 miles per hour to safely reach the other side. Some of the best scenes are of the cars racing across the top of a stadium and on the roof of the Fiat factory.

Once the gang escapes the city, they drive the cars inside a specially modified Harrington Legionnaire tour bus to make their way back to England. Things go awry and we are left with a cliffhanger for an ending—both figuratively and literally.

All of the Minis were destroyed in the making of the film, as were many of the Fiats and Alfa you see wrecked. A total of 16 Mini Coopers were used in making the movie. The Jaguar and Aston Martin were repaired and are in England today. In fact, the E-Type roadster was documented as just the 12th roadster built.

As for the Muira, if you watch closely you can see that it is a fake and has no running gear as it tumbles down the mountain.

Gone in 60 Seconds (1974)

H.B. Halicki Mercantile Co.
Director: H. B. Toby Halicki
Starring: H. B. Toby Halicki, Marion Busia, Jerry Daugirda, James McIntire, George Cole, Parnelli Jones, Gary Bettenhausen, and Eleanor

Let's face it—were it not for an incredible 40-minute chase scene that demolished countless cars, this movie would not be the favorite it is today. The story is a bit tedious, the acting is sub-B movie status, and everything else is painfully 1970s camp.

But because of a chase sequence, the likes of which had never been captured on film, this movie and the man behind it will live on as legends in the movie car genre.

If it has been a while since you have seen it, the story revolves around a Los Angeles–based band of car thieves who have a hit list of 40 cars

A pair of Austin Mini Coopers make their getaway with the boosted loot of gold. The high-speed hijinx had the Minis driving through a wild variety of places during the final climactic minutes of the film. *Photofest*

The Mini Coopers drove through sewer pipes, through buildings, and even ended up on the roof of the Fiat factory in order to escape. *Photofest*

Toby Halicki was not only producer, director, star, and stunt driver of *Gone in 60 Seconds,* he also built the co-star of the movie—*Eleanor.* Here Halicki has stripped the body panels off of the Mustang in order to build an internal cage that would protect the car from the massive hits it endured in the chase scene. *Denice Halicki Collection*

There were no special effects used to make this record-setting jump. A ramp was disguised in the wreckage in the center of the street that propelled *Eleanor* and her helmetless driver 30 feet into the air and then land 128 feet down the road. Thanks to the internal cage, Eleanor was able to drive away from this scene and Halicki was able to walk away. *Denice Halicki Collection*

Eleanor as she looked the day she was purchased. This is the one and only car used in the 40-minute chase scene, and it still runs today. Eleanor is owned by Denice Halicki, and both ladies make appearances at car shows and special events around the country. *Denice Halicki Collection*

to steal in 48 hours. All of the cars are coded with ladies names like "Janet" and, of course, "Eleanor" so the thieves can radio back to a woman named Pumpkin to cross another car off the list. Pumpkin tracks all of this on a large, wall-mounted blackboard behind her desk.

Each of the bushy-haired, sideburned larcenists carry an attaché case with the neatly arranged tools of the trade, including slide hammers, wire cutters, police scanners, and spare license plates. We also get to see firsthand how quickly and easily a car can be stolen, yet it seems a disproportionate number of cars had the keys left in them, perhaps to speed up the story.

We see them boost a Pantera, Cadillac limousine, Dodge Charger, Stutz Blackhawk, Manta, and several Rolls-Royces, including one belonging to legendary racing promoter Jerry Agajanian. Racer Parnelli Jones also makes a cameo as his Baha racing truck is stolen.

The gang's attempts to steal an "Eleanor," a 1973 Ford Mustang Mach 1, are thwarted throughout the film, and they even have to put one back to avoid getting caught.

Throughout all the thievery there is internal strife within the gang concerning who is to be the leader. As the leadership clash comes to a boil,

one of the rivals tips off the police that our "hero" (Halicki) is going for the last car: *Eleanor*.

In the midst of poaching a canary yellow 1973 Ford Mustang, the police close in, resulting in the infamous 40 minutes of nonstop chasing and crashing across greater Los Angeles.

Amazingly, there was but one car and one driver throughout the entire scene. While kudos go to Toby Halicki for producing, directing, and starring in the film, his real skills were in the choreography of the entire chase sequence, in which he did all of his own driving. There are few jump cuts where the action is not fluid, but if you watch closely you'll see where a couple of edits were done out of sequence as dents disappear and then reappear.

Just as there was only one man behind the wheel, there was but one *Eleanor*. The yellow 1973 Mustang with license plate 614 HSO was beaten and battered but kept on going. This was the last of the big Mustangs as well as the end of the fastback styling, known as the "SportsRoof" in Ford jargon.

Eleanor had a 351-ci Windsor V-8 with a four-barrel carburetor and a Cruisamatic transmission. Over 250 man hours were spent removing all of the body panels to build an internal roll cage behind the fenders, inside the car, and in the trunk. The transmission was held firm with a chain and the undercarriage was covered in 3-inch steel plating.

Halicki was strapped in with a full racing harness and had control of individually locking rear brakes.

Ninety-three cars were wrecked in the chase sequence but *Eleanor* survived every hit and was even able to drive away from the 128-foot jump under her own power.

Eleanor is still around today, replete with all the dents and battle scars from the epic chase. The car is in the hands of Denice Halicki and still occasionally appears at shows and in museums. Tragically, Toby Halicki was killed in an accident while filming a *Gone in 60 Seconds* sequel in 1989. Again he was doing all of his own stunt driving.

In 2000, Nicolas Cage and Angelina Jolie teamed up for a remake of the Halicki classic. Unfortunately, this Jerry Bruckheimer production/Touchstone Pictures film directed by Dominic Sena did not live up to the anticipation created in the promotional trailers.

This time the story is about Randall "Memphis" Raines (Cage), a California car thief of legendary repute who is called out of retirement to save his brother. Seems his brother got mixed up with some very nasty thieves while trying to follow in his older sibling's shoes.

Toby Halicki with a makeshift support structure to hold the camera inside of *Eleanor*. *Denice Halicki Collection*

However, Younger Brother bungles the boost, so Raines has to come out of retirement and steal 50 cars within 24 hours to save his brother from execution.

A great deal of the movie is spent watching Cage put his den of thieves back together for one last big job. Among the gang members are his former mentor and chop-shop-proprietor-turned-legit-bodyman Robert Duvall and love-interest Angelina Jolie, who also gave up auto theft to become a part-time bartender/part-time Ferrari mechanic.

They go about boosting a host of Ferraris, Jaguars, Mercedes-Benzs, Cadillacs, and Humvees with relative ease. Finally we get to the 50th car: *Eleanor*. This time *Eleanor* is personified in the form of a gun-metal gray 1967 Shelby GT 500 Mustang with custom bodywork and a nitrous kit.

Seems our hero has never successfully stolen one of these, and there is a poor attempt to build some suspense as our hero goes for the last heist with little time to spare.

Not only is the ensuing chase far shorter than the original, but it also lacks good direction and choreography. Just a handful of police vehicles are destroyed, and the Mustang escapes with minor scratches even after a impossible and implausible jump. Nothing even close to the feats of the original *Eleanor*.

There was one actual 1967 Shelby GT 500 custom used in the film for the close-ups and beauty shots. Twelve 1967 and 1968 Mustangs were fitted with fiberglass bodywork to replicate the actual GT 500 for the chase sequences and the big jump.

Eleven of the cars used in the film had Ford 289-ci V-8s, but one had a crate 351-ci plant that pumped out 400 horsepower to provide more oomph for the chase.

Two of the *Eleanors* were destroyed making the jump scene and a third was cut up for filming close-ups and other sequences. The rest survived.

Cage did a bit of the driving for the close-up sequences but the majority of the work was handled by Bill Young's Precision Driving Team.

Smokey and the Bandit (1977)

Universal Pictures
Director: Hal Needham
Starring: Burt Reynolds, Sally Field, Jerry Reed, and Jackie Gleason

Who would have guessed that one of the highest grossing films of the year would have been a 90-minute chase scene? Had it not been for the release of *Star Wars*, *Smokey and the Bandit* may well have been the top box office draw for 1977.

The premise of the film was really quite simple: a 90-minute, stunt-filled chase scene. The story line behind it is redneck Texas Sheriff Buford T. Justice (Jackie Gleason) chasing cocky car jockey "the Bandit" (Burt Reynolds) across the South. The high-speed hijinx relied on the popularity of Burt Reynolds and the CB radio along with some outstanding stunt work.

Smokey and the Bandit was the directorial debut of master stuntman Hal Needham. In true-to-form Needham style, the film was jam-packed with vehicular visual effects that had audiences hooting and hollering from theater balconies.

Behind all the chasing and crashing was a subplot that does have some bearing on the story. Big Enus Burdette (classic Pat McCormick) challenges Reynolds and Jerry Reed to get 200 cases of Coors beer for a party. The trick is: A) they have to go from Atlanta to Texarkana and back in 28 hours, and B) in 1977 Coors beer wasn't sold east of the Mississippi, so in effect they were bootlegging. Reynolds runs blocker in a 1977 Special Edition Pontiac Trans Am while Reed drives a spectacularly painted Peterbuilt semi truck. Along the way Reynolds picks up runaway bride Sally Field, who is being pursued by her dopey betrothed (Mike Henry) and father-in-law Gleason.

The film was a box office smash, grossing over $100 million. It also turned out to be a pay-per-view advertisement sponsored by Pontiac as the Trans Am turned out to be the unsuspecting costar.

The story itself was written before the feature car was selected. Even the original movie poster does not show the Trans Am. The choice of the Trans Am came about through the fortuitous friendship of Hal Needham and Pontiac public relations man Jim Graham.

Graham, who was in charge of Pontiac advertising and auto shows, was well known in Hollywood circles. Graham invited Needham and Reynolds to Road Atlanta while the two were scouting film locations in Georgia. Pontiac was holding closed territory meetings showing its dealers the new 1977 lineup including the Trans Am.

The 1977 Pontiac Trans-Am makes its stunning debut in *Smokey and the Bandit* as Burt Reynolds drives it out of the back of the semi truck. Pontiac invited Reynolds and director Hal Needham to see the car while on location in Georgia. The success of the film helped to double Trans-Am sales. *Photofest*

The car featured the all-new "T-Top" removable roof panels and the special black-and-gold trim package. The T-Top was the mid-1970s solution to the defunct convertible, and the gold trim package was making its first appearance as an optional trim item.

According to Pontiac's chief of design, John Schinella, GM Vice President Bill Mitchell had always liked the paint scheme on the Lotus Formula One car sponsored by John Player tobacco and asked Schinella and his team to come up with a car that looked equally as good. Schinella's answer was the Special Edition gold striping package on the black car. The gold bird that blanketed the hood was already part of the Trans Am option list.

Needham and Reynolds tried out the car and loved it. Without a second thought they slotted the new model for the film.

In retrospect there were really only two other choices of available American cars that would fill the bill at the time: Camaro and Corvette.

The mid-1970s Camaros did not have the performance panache of the Trans Am and even the once-mighty Camaro Z28 was merely a decal package by 1977.

The Corvette was certainly worthy of the mantle, but one could argue the Corvette was a little too Euro-centric for a film taking place in the deep southern United States.

Unfortunately, when Needham and Reynolds were ready to begin shooting the film, Pontiac was not up to full production capacity on the new car, so they ended up using all of the prototypes and test "mule" cars that Schinella's team had.

There is not a specific tally of how many cars were used, but most sources seem to settle on six black Trans Ams.

The cars had both manual and automatic transmissions, which can be spotted via soundtrack and by how the cars behave under acceleration. All of the cars had the 400-ci motor with the four-barrel carburetor. It is hard to believe that factory horsepower output for the 400-ci was rated at just 200.

The 1977 model was so new when filming began that they had to use the test mule cars because Trans-Am production was not under way. A total of six cars were used for the film and they all took some serious punishment. *Photofest*

Spectacular jumps like this destroyed several of the cars in the first film. In the 1980 sequel, a Turbo V-6 Trans-Am was used; it had the same body shell with the exception of a different hood. The sequel was not nearly as successful as the first film. *Photofest*

Six Pontiac Trans-Ams were used in the making of the film. This scene explains why some of the cars did not survive as this one demolishes a row of mailboxes alongside the road. *Photofest*

Some cars were modified for various stunts, for example, changing the brake bias to allow the rear wheels to lock up first and make the car easier to spin.

Two of the prototype cars were destroyed, one in the jump over the bridge, the other in the jump over the hedge.

All of the big-screen antics helped make the Trans-Am into one of the most popular cars in the United States. Sales of the cars jumped from 46,000 units in 1976 to 68,000 units in 1977 and 93,000 in 1978.

The downside to all of this success was that a handful of overly exuberant but intellectually clouded souls tried to mimic what they had seen Burt Reynolds do with the car on the big screen.

In the end Pontiac settled a number of lawsuits out of court for undisclosed sums.

In an ill-fated attempt to strike gold again, cast and director were reunited for *Smokey and the Bandit II* in 1980. This time the car was a 1980 Turbo Trans Am but the story was very weak, lacking any good stunts, or laughs for that matter. There was enough of a bond between the carmaker and movie maker for Reynolds to pose in his Bandit attire for the Pontiac sales brochures in 1980.

The Smokey series slid further in 1983, sans Reynolds and Needham. *Smokey and the Bandit III* was a total debacle with a misguided story line as Jerry Reed played the role of Bandit. Again the Turbo Trans Am was the featured car.

Comedian Jackie Gleason was at home in his role as Texas Sheriff Buford T. Justice pursuing the "Bandit" in the black Trans-Am. Virtually all of the police vehicles in the film were Pontiac Le Mans cars. *Photofest*

A Series II E-Type Jaguar painted with the Union Jack was dubbed *Shaguar* for the Austin Powers films. *Photofest*

Roll Call:
Other Notable Cops-and-Robbers Films

The Driver (1978)
Getaway driver Ryan O'Neal proves worthy adversary for police. Great chases and a very memorable sequence as he shreds a Mercedes-Benz in a parking garage.

Cobra (1986)
Sly Stallone is an ultracool tough guy assigned to protect Brigitte Nielsen while driving an impregnable 1950 Mercury hot rod. Four cars were built by Eddie Paul to survive unbelievable spins, jumps, and stunts.

Batman Movies: Batman (1989) and Batman Returns (1992)
In the two films starring Michael Keaton (1989 and 1992), two cars were built from Chevrolet Impala chassis. The wheelbase was stretched to 114 inches and mounts for the 327-ci V-8 were lowered 12 inches to allow for the low fiberglass body to fit over it. The central shape was modeled from a Rolls-Royce jet engine.

Austin Powers: International Man of Mystery (1997)
Mike Meyers stars in groovy spy send-up of 1960s espionage films. He cruises in his Series II E-Type *Shaguar*, painted with the Union Jack. Yea, baby.

Mark Hamill and Annie Potts perched atop the title star of the film, *Corvette Summer.* The very customized 1975 Corvette was designed by art director James Shoppe and built by customizer Richard Korkes. *Everett Collection*

CHAPTER 4

Hot Rods, Hippies, and Hoodlums

Motion picture studios anguish over props and costumes to help develop the look and feel of the characters in their films. Think of Marlon Brando in his T-shirt and leather jacket. Sure he looked tough, but he really became a rebel only after they put him on a Triumph motorcycle. The same goes for the films in this chapter.

Each and every car was carefully chosen to accentuate the lead characters on the screen. George Lucas is known for being a visionary and stickler for detail. For *American Graffiti* he had the 1932 Ford coupe used in the film repainted and fitted with period-correct accessories, right down to the handmade chrome headers. That car made Milner's character.

Similarly, would *Easy Rider* have been nearly as poignant if Peter Fonda had not gone to such great lengths to create the bikes?

The appearance of each of these cars, every detail, is part of the film's character development. If the character is rough and gritty, as in *Two Lane Blacktop*, then the car is finished in primer. But if the character is sharp and showy like Martin Sheen in *The California Kid*, the car is spit-shined and tricked-out. And if the character is stupid, you get the car from *Corvette Summer*.

Easy Rider (1969)

Columbia Pictures
Director: Dennis Hopper
Starring: Peter Fonda, Dennis Hopper, Jack Nicholson, Karen Black, Antonio Mendoza, Luke Askew, and Phil Spector

Easy Rider is a biker film that breaks out of the biker film mold. It is probably the most-watched film of its genre and, while its central characters are bikers, it captured the mood of the nation as the 1960s drew to a close, a time when many found their idealistic dreams dashed. On top of all that, it turned the movie industry upside down, sending just about every studio scrambling to replicate its formula.

The movie was completed with a budget of under $400,000, yet it came off as a stylish, big-budget picture on the screen thanks to the cinematography of Laszlo Kovacs, who provided a vivid American landscape as a backdrop for the believable story.

Written by Peter Fonda, Dennis Hopper, and Terry Southern, the story is encapsulated in the promotional line from the movie posters: "A man went looking for America and couldn't find it anywhere." The "man" is Wyatt (Fonda) who, along with his buddy Billy (Hopper), leaves Los Angeles behind. The pair climb aboard their Harley-Davidson choppers and go in search of the "real America." Of course their motorcycles were acquired through smuggling drugs across the Mexican border.

Their adventures while riding across the southern United States on their way to Mardi Gras in New Orleans are steeped with timely symbolism, expressed in the people they meet and the places they go.

Take, for example, their names—Wyatt and Billy—two well-known American frontier cowboy names from a simpler and freer time. And they are on motorcycles, the modern-day horses, an allegory graphically illustrated as Wyatt repairs a flat tire in the foreground while a man shoes his horse in the background.

Four Harley-Davidson Panheads were used to make the two famous bikes for *Easy Rider*. Peter Fonda purchased a 1950, two 1951s, and a 1952; they were customized by Cliff Boss to Fonda's specification. *Everett Collection*

Along the way they pick up George (Nicholson), a drunken, burnt-out lawyer torn between new ideals and the old guard. George's insights into what makes a man free are made more poignant when he meets his doom shortly thereafter.

The allegorical elements of the film carry through every scene, right down to the final image of the riderless red-white-and-blue motorcycle catapulting through the air and left burning in the ditch.

In the aftermath, both motorcycles used in the film became as big of celebrities as did their riders. In fact, they may be the most recognized and duplicated motorcycles in history.

The look and style of the bikes came from Fonda, who owned the bikes and had them customized to his suiting. There were actually four bikes used in the production, all of which

Fonda purchased at a police auction. All were Harley-Davidson Panheads: a 1950, two 1951s, and a 1952.

Fonda wanted to capture the popular chopper styling of the day so he took them to motorcycle gang member Cliff Boss to chop them.

Fonda's bike was far more radically modified. He was a veteran rider while Hopper was relatively inexperienced. The bike, dubbed *Captain America*, had a chromed wishbone rigid frame with the front end raked out to 43 degrees and 12-inch-over fork featuring turned-down lower legs. There was no front brake. Up top was a "dogbone" riser and ape-hanger handlebars.

Just about every component on the bike was chromed, including the radically upswept fishtail exhaust pipes. The finishing touches were the Paughco sissy bar and the 2-gallon peanut tank

Captain America had a chromed wishbone rigid frame with the front end raked out to 43 degrees with 12 inches over on the forks and turned-down lower legs. There was no front brake. Up top was a "dogbone" riser and ape-hanger handlebars. Hopper's Billy Bike was also a wishbone rigid frame but painted bright red. The front end was only mildly raked, and the handlebars received a modest rise. The front wheel retained the fender and drum brake. *Everett Collection*

painted in the image of the American flag. An open-faced helmet was painted to match the tank and perched defiantly atop the sissy bar.

Hopper's Billy Bike was also a wishbone rigid frame, but painted bright red. The front end was only mildly raked and the handlebars received a modest rise. The front wheel retained the fender and drum brake.

The Panhead engine and straight pipes were chrome, and the peanut tank was red with yellow flames.

Two of each bike were built, and Fonda spent a great deal of time riding them around Los Angeles to break them in and to give them a more seasoned look for the film.

The bikes rode in a trailer when they were not in use, and while on location the bikes were maintained by stuntman Tex Hall and future *The Life and Times of Grizzly Adams* (1977-1978) TV star Dan Haggerty. The actual riding sequences were quite hard on the bikes. In order for Kovacs to capture the postcard-esque scenery, the two stars were only able to run at about 30 miles per hour before the bikes would begin to overheat. Fonda could often be seen on high-speed runs to cool the bikes down after director Hopper said "cut."

As the film was nearing completion, three of the four bikes were stolen from a garage. Only one *Captain America* remained and was used for the final crash scene and was burned during filming. The three bikes were never recovered. Haggerty rebuilt the remaining bike and kept it until 1996, when it was auctioned off. It is now on display at the Alamo Car Museum in New Braunfels, Texas.

Two-Lane Blacktop (1971)
Universal Pictures
Director: Monte Hellman
Starring: James Taylor, Dennis Wilson, Warren Oates, Harry Dean Stanton, and Laurie Bird

If ever there was a cult car film, this is it. It is a road film; it is a buddy film; it is an art film. There are many reasons to debate whether or not this was meant to be an automotive version of *Easy Rider,* but there is no clear answer. What is clear is that this is an artsy B-movie packed with attitude, heavy on cinematography but light on dialog.

Singer James Taylor plays "The Driver," the pilot of a hotted-up, primer-gray 1955 Chevrolet 150 sedan. He and his buddy, "The Mechanic," played by Beach Boys drummer Dennis Wilson, cruise from town to town goading other hot rod owners into races in an attempt to earn enough money to survive. About midway through the film they meet "The Girl" (Laurie Bird) who inexplicably climbs into their car. Then one day while getting gas the trio cross paths with a self-conflicted Warren Oates driving a yellow 1970 Pontiac GTO. In the credits he is known simply as "GTO."

A lot of attitude goes back and forth between the men, and Oates quickly takes a dislike to Taylor and Wilson. The rest of the film is a two-car cross-country drag race for pink slips.

If you were to draw any parallels to *Easy Rider* you could compare the moodiness of the two films. However, *Blacktop* simply does not capture the spirit of the era as well. None of the characters have names, and there are plenty of pregnant pauses—it appears Driver and Mechanic have run out of things to say to each other.

On top of all that, it was a commercial and critical flop when it was released. It faded into obscurity for several decades and only recently has it become available on videotape. Either you love it or you hate it.

As for the cars in the film, three identical Chevrolet 150s were built for the movie by Richard Ruth of Competition Engineering in Sunland, California. Two cars were built for filming with a third stunt car that was never used. The stunt car was not actually drivable but featured a full roll cage for a scripted rollover scene that was never filmed.

The car had a lift-off fiberglass hood-fender assembly held in place by pins. The trunk lid was also fiberglass as were the doors, which had Plexiglas windows. The rear wheelwells were radiused, and the car had chrome reverse rims with baby moon lug covers. The rest of the chrome was removed from the car.

Under the hood was a 454-ci big-block Chevy with two four-barrel carburetors perched atop a high-rise tunnel-ram manifold. Four-inch, handmade headers rounded out the package. Power was fed through a four-speed transmission. A special tube axle with coil-over shocks was fabricated for the front suspension.

Warren Oates drove a 455-ci Pontiac that was pretty much street stock and finished in creamy yellow.

After production on *Blacktop* was completed, the badly bruised and beaten Chevrolets remained on call with the studio. Approximately a year or so later a casting call went out for hot rods for a new film. The two cars were roughed up pretty badly in the filming, so the best parts of the two film cars were melded into one for use in the 1973 blockbuster *American Graffiti.*

The black Chevrolet crashed in the Paradise Road drag scene in the first *Grafitti* film, so it did not appear in the 1979 sequel. Three years after the first film the car was purchased from the transportation supervisor. It has since changed hands three times and is now with a private collector on the East Coast.

Vanishing Point (1971)
20th Century Fox
Director: Richard C. Sarafian
Starring: Barry Newman, Cleavon Little, Dean Jagger, Paul Kosko, Severn Darden, and Gilda Texter

This is another low-budget, one-man-against-the-world film that achieved cult-classic status virtually overnight. *Vanishing Point* was originally released with little fanfare and subsequently vanished from theaters almost as quickly as it arrived.

Barry Newman in a rare moment outside of the car in *Vanishing Point* **as he tangles with a rattlesnake in the desert.** *Photofest*

However, when it became a big hit in Europe the movie was re-released as a drive-in double-feature with *The French Connection*. Many know of it, but little is known about it.

The story is about a car jockey named Kowalski (Newman) who shuttles cars around the country. He takes a bet that he can deliver a 1970 Dodge Challenger from Denver to San Francisco in 15 hours. Naturally it is not long before the police get involved and the film develops into a cross-country chase.

As the chase wears on, a blind radio DJ named Super Soul (Little) supplies Kowalski with important information that he picks up from police radio transmissions. The music he plays provides the backdrop for some of the chase sequences, but his performance is borderline blacksploitation.

Kowalski, who we learn about through a series of flashbacks, encounters an interesting variety of folks along the way, including a snake worshiper, some stupid hitchhikers, and a nude female dirt bike enthusiast.

In the dramatic final scene Kowalski drives head-on into a roadblock comprised of two very large bulldozers. You can take it as a 90-minute dramatic chase film, or you can get lost in the message and symbolism of the anti-hero and his defiant ways that mirror the allegorical content of *Easy Rider.*

The story was inspired by the true story of a driver who refused to stop and perished in a California roadblock. The car for the film was not specified in the script. It was chosen by Carey Loftin, stunt coordinator for the movie. In a 1986 interview, Loftin said he chose the car because of its rugged suspension and horsepower.

John Milner's yellow coupe in *American Graffiti* was a chopped five-window 1932 Ford with a small-block V-8, Man-A-Fre four-twos manifold, Stromberg carbs, and handmade exhaust headers. Falfa's Chevy was a black 1955 that came from the film *Two Lane Blacktop.* The car had a 454 V-8 with a high-rise manifold and two four-barrel carburetors. *Everett Collection*

Chrysler supplied five 1970 Alpine White Challengers to the production company in exchange for the ubiquitous promotional consideration. After the film was completed the cars were returned to Chrysler.

Four of the cars had 440-ci engines with four-barrel carburetors and four-speed transmissions. The fifth car had a 383-ci powerplant with an automatic transmission.

There were references in the film to the cars being supercharged, but the cars were left stock, with the exception of stiffer shocks bolted into the car used in the creek-jumping scene.

Loftin did nearly all of the driving in the film and certainly all of the stunts. Newman drove the car in the straight-line speed runs and for the close-ups.

In order to give the illusion of very high speeds, Loftin and Newman typically drove the desert roads at 80–90 miles per hour. The cameras were "undercranked," or slowed down, to further enhance the sensation of speed when the film was run at regular speed.

The stunt car used for the final crash was actually an already-trashed 1967 Chevrolet Camaro that was painted white and stripped of its engine and gearbox. The nose of the Camaro was packed with explosives and a cable was connected to the front suspension. The cable was threaded between the bulldozers and the other was tied to the rear of the 383-equipped Challenger. Loftin towed the Camaro at 80 miles per hour to achieve maximum effect for the final scene of the movie.

Charles Martin Smith in a white 1958 Chevrolet Bel Air that he spends most of the movie trying not to dent.
Everett Collection

American Graffiti (1973)

Universal Studios
Director: George Lucas
Starring: Richard Dreyfuss, Ron Howard, Paul LeMat, Charlie Martin Smith, Cindy Williams, Candy Clark, Harrison Ford, Mackenzie Phillips, Suzanne Somers, and Wolfman Jack

In 1971 a fledgling filmmaker named George Lucas released a futuristic science fiction film called THX 1138. The Orwellian tale of a bland society where everyone looked the same was visually impactful but a box office disaster.

Despite those dismal results Lucas was given another chance to direct with a comedy-drama called *American Graffiti* that he had written along with Gloria Katz and William Huyck. With a modest budget of $750,000, Lucas set out to tell the coming-of-age story of a group of high school students out for a night of fun on their last evening together before leaving for college. Filmed in just 25 days, the movie went on to gross nearly $100 million and earned Lucas an Academy Award nomination.

The entire story takes place during a California summer night in 1962 and principally focuses on the characters played by Richard Dreyfuss and Ron Howard. Each has his own story line. Howard decides his future with his girlfriend (Cindy Willams) while Dreyfuss is smitten by a blond (Suzanne Somers) driving a white 1956 Ford Thunderbird and spends the rest of the night trying to find her.

Meanwhile, Howard loans his beloved 1958 Chevrolet to a friend (Charles Martin Smith) who is trying to impress a girl. Another friend (Paul LeMat) is stuck babysitting Mackenzie Phillips while cruising in his yellow 1932 Ford five-window hot rod.

Everyone in the movie is listening to legendary radio DJ Wolfman Jack, who spins famous music from the 1950s and early 1960s.

Lucas' poignant and highly entertaining story flawlessly captured the era, and it made hot rods and cruising fashionable once again.

Just like the story line, there were two, perhaps three, automotive stars in the film. We saw a lot of the white 1958 Chevrolet Bel Air as Smith

The famous yellow Ford coupe and 1955 Chevrolet at the drive-in prior to the final drag-racing showdown. *Everett Collection*

tries not to hurt it or puke in it. While it is a nice car, it does not do anything of particular note.

The real car star of the film is the bright yellow 1932 Ford five-window hot rod driven throughout the film by the bellicose Paul LeMat. For many, the car is known simply as "Milner's coupe," taken from the name of LeMat's character, John Milner.

Lucas' script called for a fenderless, chopped street rod for the character to drive. The production team went out and found a group of hot rods for George Lucas to choose from. The final choice was a $1,300 red, full-fendered hot rod, chosen mainly because the top was already chopped.

Lucas was very specific in the details of how the car was to look. The hood was removed; the front fenders were removed and the rears bobbed. The grille was sectioned and the entire front-end assembly was chrome-plated. A special set of headers were fitted, and finally the car was painted with many coats of canary yellow.

The '32 was perched on blackwall tires mounted on silver reverse rims. Lucas always carries something over from his previous films, so this car was given California plate THX 138 from his 1970 debut movie.

Milner's coupe was powered by a small-block Ford engine with a Man-A-Fre four-twos manifold and Stromberg carburetors. The open and exposed chrome sidepipes ran back along each side of the car to the middle of the doors. Power was fed through a four-speed ST10 transmission. The car had no fusebox or electrical panel.

Milner's archrival in the film is brash cowboy Bob Falfa (Harrison Ford), driving a black 1955 Chevrolet 150 sedan. This car has a movie pedigree: It was one of the three Chevy's built for the film *Two-Lane Blacktop.*

The gray primer was painted over with black, and a hood scoop was placed on the one-piece, lift-off hood-and-fender assembly. The

Charles Martin Smith and Candy Clark in a scene with one of the automotive extras from the film. *Everett Collection*

trunk lid was also a removable fiberglass panel but used hinges instead of the pins used in Black-top. A bench seat replaced the buckets and the fiberglass doors were replaced with stock doors, but the roll bar remained in place.

The car looked very stylish and period-correct on the chrome reverse rims with baby moon center caps. The radiused rear fenders completed the look.

The third and unused stunt car from Black-top was used for the big crash scene while a junk-yard-sourced 1955 was used for the burn scene.

Under the hood is a 454 cubic inch V8 with a high-rise manifold and dual four-barrel carburetors hooked up to a four-speed transmission and posi-rear end.

After the movie and its poor and forgettable 1979 sequel, *More American Graffiti,* Milner's coupe sat on the studio lot while the black Chevy languished in the front yard of the film's transportation supervisor. After about one year, a collector from Wichita, Kansas, purchased both cars from the studio in a sealed bid auction He kept the cars for several years before selling the Chevrolet to a private party in Maryland while the Ford went to a collector in northern California.

The Chevy was in showable condition, but the Ford required a bit of restoration to make it drivable. Even so, the only real work done to the

Ford was the replacement of the four-two manifold. Everything else remains as it was in the film.

The owner of the Chevrolet removed the roll bar and installed a full leather interior along with a stock 1955 steering wheel.

The California Kid (1974)
ABC and Universal Pictures
Richard T. Heffron
Starring: Martin Sheen, Vic Morrow, Michelle Phillips, Nick Nolte, and Stuart Margolin

The California Kid transcends the cult-classic category and leaps into all-time favorite status. Sure, the story is simple and predictable, but the cars and the location make it nearly timeless. Unfortunately, this one is seldom aired, and since it was a made-for-TV movie it is not available on video.

The California Kid was shot just 45 miles north of Los Angeles, in Piru, California, in the spring of 1974. The late Vic Morrow costarred as lawman-gone-bad Sheriff Roy. Apparently the embittered sheriff was quite intolerant of speeders and weary of handing out tickets. Instead of pulling the violators over and writing a citation, he pushed them over—over a cliff that is.

As the story unfolds we witness Sheriff Roy chase several hot rods and musclecars along the treacherous California canyon roads where he

In 1999 the *California Kid* celebrated the 25th anniversary of the movie and returned to the original location in Piru, California. This is likely how the car looked on the first day of filming. *Tony Thacker*

eventually bumps them off the edge as they over-cook the infamous "Clarksburg" curve. Through the story we learn about seven of the sheriff's victims.

Enter Martin Sheen, the mysterious stranger whose presence in town is about as subtle as Arnold Schwarzenegger at a midget convention. Sheen rolled into the one-horse berg driving a liquidy-black 1934 Ford three-window coupe bedecked with bright orange flames on the hood and fenders. The words "California Kid" were scribed on the doors.

Sheen's character was the older brother of Morrow's most recent victim and in town to investigate his sibling's accident. During the rest of the film Sheen and Morrow play a cat-and-mouse game while Sheen also plays house with cafe waitress Michelle Phillips.

Finally "the Kid" bates the sheriff into a high-speed canyon chase where he turns the tables on the sheriff who plunges off the Clarksburg curve to his death. The Kid avenges the death of his brother and frees the townfolk of Sheriff Roy's tyranny, then drives out of town into the sunset.

The film was the catalyst that set the hot rodding careers of Pete Chapouris and Jim "Jake" Jacobs on fire by showcasing the flamed Ford street rod. However, neither the car nor the men ever intended to become such recognizable celebrities in the hot rod world.

The Kid was Chapouris' creation, which he started to build in 1973 after tiring of his T-bucket. He bought the car for $250 mostly intact with the top already raked and chopped, but it did not have fenders or paint. The car is all Ford, through and through: 1948 Ford brakes, 1936 axle housings, 1968 Mustang steering gear, and a 1968 302-ci Ford engine under the severely louvered hood.

The thin-walled 302 was extensively reworked with TRW pistons, Mellings lifters and camshaft, 11:1 heads, Offenhauser intake, and 650-cfm Holley carburetor. The power runs through a rare 1968 Ford C8 transmission and 1936 Ford rear end with Halibrand quickie.

Shortly after he started work on the car, well-known hot rod writer Gray Baskerville called wanting to feature the car in a comparison with Jake's 1934 Ford coupe in the November 1973 issue of *Rod & Custom* magazine. Not only were the cars to be featured inside the magazine, but they were also featured on the cover.

That issue of the magazine introduced Pete and Jake to the world (and to each other); it also led to another fortuitous call, this time from TV producer Howie Horwitz of Batman fame. Horwitz asked Chapouris to bring the car to Universal Studios right away so they could see the car in person and perhaps use it in a film that was to begin shooting in mere days. Horwitz and company fell for the car on the spot. As it turns out, the project was moving so quickly that Chapouris had to leave the car behind and hitch a ride home so filming could commence immediately.

The producers loved the car, but you would not have known it from their treatment of the machine. Unlike most movie stars who are pampered on the set, the *Kid* was used, abused, and beat up pretty badly. There were a number of stunt scenes that called for the car to slide and spin, but the car gripped the road too well. Stunt driver Gerry Summers needed help to break the rear end loose, so he spun the car in sand and gravel that scarred the paint. The tires were all chunked and the left front tire was blown and the rim bent.

Also, a light fell from a stand, denting the grille, and both side windows were shattered from repeated door slamming. When Pete got the car back there were footprints on the tops of the fenders, and Dale Caulfield's brilliant paintwork was destroyed. Fortunately, the studio paid Pete to put the car back the way they got it.

Today the car is in the hands of a private collector and looks just as good as the day Chapouris first built it. In 1999 the Kid and its creator were reunited in Piru to celebrate the 25th anniversary of the film.

Corvette Summer (1978)

MGM/United Artists
Director: Matthew Robbins
Starring: Mark Hamill, Annie Potts, Eugene Roche, Danny Bonaduce, and Kim Milford

This is a love-it-or-hate-it film. No, there is nothing to love about Mark Hamill's acting nor is there anything endearing about the ridiculous and implausible story. You either love the radically customized Corvette or you see it as the ugliest thing on four wheels.

The car is the on-screen creation of Ken Dantley (Hamill), a greasy devotee to high school shop class. He and his classmates purchased and repaired a wrecked 1975 Corvette. But this was not a mere restoration; rather, it was a massive makeover.

Shortly after the car is completed it is stolen by professional car thieves from Las Vegas. The impetuous Dantley has developed an emotional attachment to the car and sets out to retrieve it against his shop teacher's wishes.

The rest of the film is a series of events that keep him from his quarry. Finally Dantley is be-friended by, and falls in love with, hooker-wannabe, Vanessa (Annie Potts) in her oh-so-1970s conversion van. In the end he gets the car and the girl.

The actual car was a one-of-a-kind custom penned by art director James Shoppe and built by customizer Richard Korkes. It started out as a 1975 Corvette Stingray with T-Tops. Korkes gave it a facelift with a one-piece fiberglass hood featuring exposed headlights and a massive, louvered bulge at the center. Outboard chrome headers and sidepipes emerged just behind the front wheels. The rear fascia got new taillights, spoiler, and a giant Chevrolet bow tie with the large Stingray script at the center.

If all that, the fender flairs, and metallic-flake red paint were not enough, the car was also converted to right-hand drive.

Most agree that the car and the film are equally forgettable.

Roll Call: Other Notable Hot Rods, Hippie, and Hoodlum Films

Thunder Road (1958)

Robert Mitchum is a moonshiner driving and crashing a variety of Fords.

Rendezvous (1965)

The best nine minutes of in-car footage ever recorded. French director Claude Lelouch straps a camera on the hood of a Ferrari 275 GTB as F1 driver Maurice Trintignant drives flat-out across Paris early on a Sunday morning. A truly wild ride. Turn it up!

Fireball 500 (1966)

Frankie and Annette haul moonshine in a zany Barris-built stock car called SSXR. The car started as a 1966 Plymouth Barracuda, the top was cut off, and a 400 horsepower, 426-ci mill was stuffed under the hood.

Dirty Mary, Crazy Larry (1974)

Peter Fonda is a minor-league racer who dreams of the big time but needs financing. He and Susan George rip off the dough, and then it's off to the chases in a 1969 Dodge Charger R/T 440. Non-stop tire-squealing action, but watch for trains.

Hooper (1978)

Burt Reynolds in another buddy flick boosted by explosive stunts and a rocket-powered 1977 Pontiac Trans Am.

The Blues Brothers (1980)

John Belushi and Dan Akyroyd in a 1974 Dodge Monaco with "a cop motor, cop tires, cop suspension, cop shocks, and it was built before catalytic converters so it will run good on regular gas." Universal Studios built eight identical cars in the image of former Chicago police cruisers. Seven were destroyed during filming along with countless dozens of other Chrysler-based police cars.

Tucker: The Man and His Dream (1988)

Francis Ford Coppola bought one of the 51 Tuckers built for himself and makes an excellent film about the story of designer/builder Preston Tucker and his cars.

Thelma & Louise (1991)

Female buddy film as Susan Sarandon and Geena Davis meet their destiny in a 1966 Ford Thunderbird convertible.

CHAPTER 5

Racing

▮▮

Hollywood has a real obsession with the world of auto racing. For years they've been trying to use it as a backdrop to any number of stories, but only a few are able to pull it off.

Elvis Presley's *Viva Las Vegas* used only stock racing footage to portray him as a driver. It worked well enough, but Al Pacino never really fit the role as a Formula One driver in *Bobby Deerfield*.

Every so often an ambitious director comes along with a grand plan and a big budget. The first to do it was John Frankenheimer, who set out to make a film set against the world of Grand Prix driving. He disrupted an entire season of racing and shot thousands of feet of film that eventually won an Academy Award for cinematography. Unfortunately, his plot was thin.

Steve McQueen attempted to accomplish the same feat but set it all against one race: *Le Mans*. It was a mess from the start and never really had a script. The racing sequences were good, but there was almost no story and the film was a critical flop.

Blake Edwards used fictitious cars to make a comedy about an around-the-world race. It worked, thanks to clever gimmicks and a big cast.

Most recently Tom Cruise was cast as NASCAR driver Cole Trickle in a big-budget film, *Days of Thunder*. Only the star power of Cruise made this film work because it painted NASCAR as a nontechnical smash 'em derby.

In the end, all these films deliver some redeeming footage of great racing action.

The Great Race (1965)
Warner Bros.
Director: Blake Edwards
Starring: Tony Curtis, Jack Lemmon, Natalie Wood, Peter Falk, and Keenan Wynn

Legendary comedy filmmaker Blake Edwards had the vision of this movie in his head for at least four years before production began in 1964. Hot off his successful *A Shot in the Dark* starring Peter Sellers, Edwards set out to make this comedy-adventure about a New York-to-Paris car race set shortly after the turn of the century. Warner Bros. gave Edwards a budget of over $8 million, which was the highest in movie history at the time.

The cartoonish story was loosely (very loosely) based on the true tale of the 170-day-long New York-to-Paris race of 1908, which was won by a 1907 Thomas Flyer. Edwards' comedy spoof takes place in vaguely the same period, a time when the world was transitioning from the horse to the automobile.

Tony Curtis played Leslie Gallant III, also know as "The Great Leslie." He is a suave and debonair daredevil who always appeared in perfectly pressed white suits. His heroics lead him to the Webber Motor Car Company where he proposes a race from New York to Paris to prove the dominance of American-built automobiles. The company consents and builds him a special car, dubbed the Leslie Special, for the race.

McQueen stands alongside the Porsche 917K between takes. The film crew went to great lengths to ensure continuity within the movie. By meticulously re-creating race cars that matched those in the actual Le Mans race, they created a seamless splice between the Hollywood footage and actual race footage. *Photofest*

Tony Curtis poses alongside the Leslie Special. The car was designed and built by the Warner Brothers studios for *The Great Race.* The PVC body was mounted on a modified Ford truck frame and powered by a Ford 260 V-8 and automatic transmission. *Photofest*

The race draws a host of competitors, including the Great Leslie's archrival, the dastardly Professor Fate, played to the hilt by Jack Lemmon. The professor builds his own car from pieces stolen from the finest cars in the world. As he unveils his Hannibal Twin 8 his henchman Max (Peter Falk) is just returning from stealing a magneto from a Rolls-Royce.

The do-gooding Leslie sets out to win the race fair and square while Fate plans to cheat his way to the victory podium. After Fate dispatches the other entrants, the archrivals are continually thrust together in a series of comic circumstances until they cross the finish line in Paris.

A subplot involves the budding romance between the Great Leslie and suffragette Maggie DuBois, played by the radiant Natalie Wood. She enters the race in a Stanley Steamer as a reporter for the *New York Sentinel* but ends up in Leslie's car after tricking his manservant Hezekiah (Keenan Wynn).

In the end it appears Fate wins the race but cannot accept it because Leslie has cheated him out of the victory because he stopped just short of the finish line to profess his love for Maggie. As the story closes the two are challenged to race back to New York.

At the time the movie was made it was one of the biggest-budget comedies in history. Today it is still a respectable film, but the slapstick becomes overbearing at times.

The two main cars in the film are the Leslie Special driven by Curtis and the Hannibal Twin 8 driven by Lemmon. Both cars were built from scratch by the studio expressly for the film at a cost of over $100,000. That price tag also included a lot of spare parts to ensure there were no breaks in production.

A total of seven cars were built: three Leslie Specials and four Hannibal 8s. Two of each were complete running models and one of

Natalie Wood poses with a starting pistol as Jack Lemmon in the Hannibal Twin 8 and Tony Curtis in the Leslie Special prepare to race. Both cars featured original brass-era automobile fittings. *Photofest*

each was a lightweight shell made for static shots. The last car was a Hannibal 8 with the hydraulic scissors lift mechanism but without an engine. According to a Warner Bros. interoffice memo to Col. J. L. Warner, the cost of the cars, up to $100,000, was being billed to the Firestone Tire Company in exchange for promotional consideration in relation to the film. Firestone lettering could easily be seen on the sidewalls of the Leslie Special's tires. Final cost of the cars is estimated to be between $105,000 and $110,000.

The Warner Bros. art department designed the cars, trying to get a specific look and feel for each one. While the Leslie Special obviously got its initial cues from the Thomas Flyer, it can be said that it is an artist's hybrid conception of a sporting brass-era car. The hood and grille show elements of a Rolls-Royce Silver Ghost or Mercedes-Benz SSK while the cockpit comes from a cross between the Thomas Flyer and a Revere.

The wildly upturned fenders draw inspiration from an American Underslung.

The actual body of the Leslie Special was made of white PVC plastic mounted on a modified Ford truck frame. The fenders and running boards were constructed of metal to support camera gear as well as the actors in several scenes.

The exterior was dressed-out with a host of actual brass-era automobile fittings, right down to the bulb horn, outboard shift and brake levers, bows on the top, and the oversized headlamps. A carbide generator was mounted on the running board, but the lights were not functional.

To round out the look, bogus external exhaust pipes were added to each side of the hood, complete with leather straps and brass buckles.

The interior was all done in red vinyl. There were virtually no instruments on the dashboard, and a four-spoke Ford Model T steering wheel sat atop the brass column. A frail-looking brass lever akin to a period spark advance lever protruded

Five Hannibal Twin 8s were built by the studio. Each had a fiberglass body on a custom-made steel frame and was powered by a Volkswagen-based forklift engine and transmission. This rare rear view shows the twin radiators for the fictitious two engines. The spare tires mounted on the rear deck matched the ones mounted on the rims. *Everett Collection*

from the steering column. It was actually a clever disguise for the automatic transmission gear change.

The car utilized a leaf spring suspension with four-wheel hydraulic brakes. The red, 10-spoke front and 12-spoke rear wheels were cast in metal for safety's sake and came in at a reported $500 each. Extra wheels and tires were mounted on the rear as actual spares. The tires were period replicas of white rubber Firestone tires with the raised "nonskid" tread lettering.

A small-block Ford V-8 engine was capable of propelling the Leslie Special to nearly 100 miles per hour if anyone was brave enough to drive the plastic car that fast.

It is difficult to say that anything other than imagination inspired the car driven by Leslie's archrival. The Hannibal 8 is the embodiment of what an evil-minded professor might build at a time when there was no real form or norm for automotive design.

The six-wheeled beast had a rear engine with four drive wheels at the back and an unconventionally tall cockpit with two bench seats but only a painted outline of where the doors would actually be. There were snaps for side curtains, a windshield, and a tent-like canopy top.

The vehicle was finished all in black, naturally, and hid an arsenal of Professor Fate's villainous weaponry, including smoke screens at the rear and a cannon in the nose.

The fiberglass body was set on a custom-made, meticulously finished steel box frame. The four rear wheels were actually wooden-spoke Ford Model T wheels with the axles attached to truck-sourced leaf springs. Hydraulic disc brakes arrested the rears.

Two Hannibal Twin 8 cars were built with the ever-fascinating scissors mechanism. In its fully raised position, the body hovered 10 feet above the ground. Thanks to its hydraulic steering and specially fitted drivetrain, the car could actually be driven with the body fully extended. *Everett Collection*

This studio photograph of the Hannibal Twin 8 shows the extended cannon, tent-like top, and authentic antique car brass headlights. *Everett Collection*

The front wheels were custom-made, chrome 48-spoke wheels resembling motorcycle wheels. There was no front suspension nor front brakes. Steering was also hydraulic, directed by an original Model T wheel. The only nonhydraulic control in the car was the accelerator cable. Tires were again the Firestone "nonskid" but in black rubber, naturally.

The Hannibal 8 was powered by a Volkswagen-built, four-cylinder forklift engine and transaxle with chain drive. Because it used a forklift-based drivetrain, the car only had one forward and one reverse gear and was capable of approximately 20 miles per hour.

The interior upholstery was typical button and pleat vinyl. The dashboard was merely a row of toggle switches that allegedly triggered the Professor's tricks. A hand crank operated the single windshield wiper, and a small lever opened the panel at the front of the car to reveal the cannon. The only gauge was a brass speedometer located to the right of the steering wheel.

Like the Leslie, the exterior was finished with all sorts of original brass trim, including oversized headlamps on the end of the front fenders and brass railroad lamps on the rear.

Two cars were built with the scissors mechanism that raised and lowered the body, one with an engine and one without. Again the craftsmanship was topnotch, and the car with the engine could actually drive with the body raised as high as 10 feet.

There was a single hydraulic ram that worked much like a gas station service-bay lift to raise the body. The pump ran off of the little motor, and all of the hydraulic lines were meticulously disguised. The lift car with engine weighed over 3 tons while the nonlift cars weighed a bit less (but not by much).

Little is known about the post-film lives of the seven cars built for *The Great Race*. One Leslie Special did reappear in the 1969 western *The Good Guys and the Bad Guys*, starring Robert Mitchum and George Kennedy.

Today one Leslie Special is rumored to be in Europe. A second Leslie sold at auction in the early 1990s and is in a private collection in Indiana that also contains Jack Benny's Maxwell and a Tucker used in the film of the same name.

California-based collector David Simon purchased the motorized lift car from the estate of actor Val Kilmer's father. The car was in a gross state of disrepair, but after a several-year restoration, the car is shown on a regular basis.

Grand Prix (1966)

MGM
Director: John Frankenheimer
Starring: James Garner, Yves Montand, Eva Marie Saint, Brian Bedford, Antonio Sabato, and Jessica Walter

In 1964 film director John Frankenheimer attended the 24 Hours of Le Mans race. He was so taken by the experience it inspired him to make a film set against the world of auto racing. Obviously there were many ways he could have turned, but Frankenheimer was not one to compromise. He wanted the pinnacle of motorsports—Formula One.

Frankenheimer's goal was to capture Grand Prix motor racing as it never had been before. The ultimate objective was to put the audience in the race with a real sensation of speed.

In order to pull this off Frankenheimer, and his crew had to join the 1966 F1 season almost literally as another team. The undertaking was massive. Over 200 people plus cameras, lights, film, cars, and helicopters traveled to all six countries of the racing circuit. A huge amount of the $7 million budget was spent on the transportation of the cinematic racing team, which was a staggering sum for a noncompetitive race entry even by Formula One standards.

All of this effort and expense delivered the very realistic racing sequences that were the film's real hook. Recording the action on film was no small feat. The studios called upon NASA to help develop electronic and microwave cameras to be carried in a variety of cars and atop drivers' helmets, all of which could be easily controlled by the co-driver. A Ford GT40 and a Shelby Cobra carried cameras with sophisticated miniature control motors to aim the lens mounted on the tops, sides, and rears of the cars. The co-driver was able to see what the cameras saw via a 2-inch monitor connected to the handheld controls.

Bell Labs built a large, 16-millimeter "twin camera" that was strapped to the helmet of driver

The cast of *Grand Prix* poses at the finish line of a deserted Monza track. The fictitious competitors were the Japanese Yamura, driven by James Garner, the Manetta-Ferraris, driven by Yves Montand and Antonio Sabato, and the Jordan-BRM piloted by Brian Bedford. *Everett Collection*

Bob Bondurant with lenses flanking his head to deliver a real driver's-eye view.

As the movie entourage traveled with the F1 circus they became nothing short of a distraction to the business of the F1 competition. Drivers, teams, promoters, and the press found them disruptive because of all their special needs and desire to photograph every element on and off the track. Yet despite all of the complaining there was something exciting about Hollywood being on the scene. Many of the drivers signed on for cameo appearances, and even Henry Manney's monthly coverage of the season in *Road & Track* magazine contained an update on the filming.

World Champion (1961) Phil Hill was Frankenheimer's chief racing advisor and drove several of the camera cars. Five-time champion Juan Manuel Fangio came out of a ten-year retirement for

a brief appearance in the film and nearly caused a riot with his presence at the Monza track.

Other drivers appearing in the film were Joakim Bonnier, Bob Bondurant, Jack Brabham, Dan Gurney, Lorenzo Bandini, Jo Siffert, Chris Amon, Richie Ginther, Mike Parkes, Bruce McLaren, Peter Revson, Dennis Hulme, Jochen Rindt, and an over-emoting Graham Hill.

Once all of the hard work of capturing the action and the story line during the 1966 racing season was done, the film still required all of editing and sound work and final polish for a Christmas release. After all of the effort and anticipation, the final result was a bit disappointing.

While everyone agrees the racing footage is second to none, with perhaps the exception of Steve McQueen's *Le Mans*, the story of *Grand Prix* is too melodramatic.

Eva Marie Saint poses alongside James Garner's Formula One car with Brian Bedford in the background. The cars the actors drove in the film were actually rebodied Lotus Formula 3 cars supplied by the Jim Russell Driving School. Bogus exhaust pipes and carburetor stacks were attached to the rear cowling, and the wheels were widened by 5 inches to be proportional with the enlarged bodywork. *Everett Collection*

The plot centers around American driver Pete Aron, played by James Garner. Aron is an aggressive driver and a bit of a loner anxious to prove himself after a reckless accident with his teammate in the opening race sequence at Monaco.

Scott Stoddard, Aron's teammate, is portrayed by a perpetually moping Brian Bedford. Bedford is a haunted man. He's haunted by his injuries. He's haunted by the memory of his brother who was killed racing, and he's haunted by his failing marriage to fashion model Jessica Walter.

Meanwhile, Yves Montand portrays suave Frenchman and Manetta-Ferrari driver Jean-Pierre Sarti, who struggles with his commitment to the sport and to his wife. In the film he takes up with American journalist Eva Marie Saint despite the fact that his wife is the president of a huge automobile company and supporting his way of life.

The cast also includes Antonio Sabato as the wild, young Sicilian driver Nino Barlini, and Toshiro Mifune in his first English-speaking role as Japanese industrialist Izo Yamura.

The characters and the cars in the fictional film were completely transparent in the way they mirrored the real-life Formula One cast.

Bedford maintained his Scottish heritage and even wore a tartan band on his helmet ala Jackie Stewart, which helped the action

James Garner gets fitted for his new car at the fictitious Yamura team headquarters. Garner did most of his own driving after rigorous training at the Jim Russell school, but his driving was curtailed after the insurance company got wind of his participation. *Everett Collection*

sequences. Mifune was obviously replicating Soichiro Honda right down to the all-white cars, while Adolfo Celi put on his best Enzo Ferrari face when portraying Agostino Manetta. Finally, Jack Watson personified the emotional and hard-nosed Lotus team owner Colin Chapman.

It is worth noting that Frankenheimer's calculated choice of Mifune was worth over $3 million at the Asian market box office.

In the end Aron redeems himself with the title crown, Bedford defeats his demons, and Sarti meets his fate. All this occurs in the final lap of the final race of the season.

Factoring out the soap-opera plot, every one of the racing sequences are excellent and well deserving of the Academy Award they received for cinematography. The film also serves as an incredible document to a style and formula of rac-

ing that would otherwise only be available in books and newsreels.

Frankenheimer chronicled some incredible action, including the high banks of the now-defunct Monza track, the long-forgotten stretches of the original Spa circuit, and some brilliant drifting through the streets of Monaco. He captured an era that was all about the skill of the driver, thanks to the seemingly equal technology of the cars. Top it all off with detailed close-ups of moving suspension, spinning tachometers, crisp gear changes, and the first heel-toe action in cinema, and it is the Formula One fans' delight.

Of course, camera angles, lighting, and editing were only half of the battle for Frankenheimer. For his racing film to be totally believable his actors would need to drive actual racing cars. The director had no intention of using dummy cars against a blue

Grand Prix chronicles some of the world's greatest tracks before they were emasculated by chicanes and run-off areas. Here Garner leads the pack on the infamous high banks of the Monza track in Italy. *Everett Collection*

A candid shot of James Garner practicing in a Formula 3 Lotus. He took to the driving quickly while others such as Brian Bedford struggled mightily. Garner went on to compete professionally.

screen. Unfortunately, none of them ever had been in a racing car, and Brian Bedford did not even possess a driver's license.

Prior to the beginning of production, anyone cast as a driver was sent to the Jim Russell Driving School in England. There they were taught everything necessary to become a believable on-screen driver.

Garner grasped it immediately and did all of his own driving in the film. That was until the insurance company got wind of it, and Garner was forced to use a double or the unsavory blue-screen backdrop. Garner went on to drive professionally and control his own racing team.

Montand was able to do well enough to get through the scenes that required him to drive a car on film.

Meanwhile Bedford struggled mightily and never really came to grips with the driving portion of his role. At one point he was quoted as saying, "Asking an actor to drive Formula One is like asking Phil Hill to play Hamlet." It was fortuitous that his character spent most of his time out of the car.

The cars the actors drove in the film were actually Lotus Formula 3 cars from the Russell school, powered by English Ford 997-cc engines. Jim Russell and his brother Peter fabricated fiberglass bodywork to replicate their Formula One big brothers. The replacement bodies were authentic right down to the fake rivets.

Additional fabrications included faux exhaust pipes and carburetor intakes bent from thin aluminum tubing and fake gearboxes made from wood and sheet metal. All of these parts were interchangeable on any of the 10 cars Russell supplied for the film.

Obviously the wheels would have looked too thin, so the metal rims were sliced down the middle and 5 inches of metal was welded to the centers. All this rubber prevented the little Ford-Cosworth from spinning the real wheels on the standing starts. To add more realism, the tires were coated with oil. To finish the effect, vacuum-formed plastic wheel covers were made to replicate the wheels on the actual cars.

Russell also supplied three cars without engines to be used for any hair-raising crash sequences. Rather than risk injury to stuntmen, a steel cylinder was inserted into the rear of the

Yves Montand awaits direction as he sits on the grid in the mock Ferrari. The stars of *Grand Prix* drove Formula cars from the Jim Russell Driving School that were disguised as full-size Formula One cars with the aid of plastic bodywork and false exhaust pipes. *Photofest*

car. The cylinder was akin to the barrel of a gun but charged with compressed nitrogen. When the charge was released the car would accelerate to 100 miles per hour in approximately 15 feet. This allowed the crew to fire cars in any direction, including skyward, with intense realism. With interchangeable bodywork they could simulate the crash of any one of the competing cars.

Cameras were strapped to all of the cars to capture close-ups of the drivers at speed. Every camera had radio-controlled motors to change the angle, allowing the film crew to get good, live-action close-ups.

If you have never seen this racing epic it is well worth the three-hour investment. One final note: As actors go, Graham Hill was a great driver.

Le Mans (1971)

National General Pictures
Director: Lee H. Katzin
Starring: Steve McQueen, Siegfried Rauch, Elga Andersen, and Ronald Leigh-Hunt

This is the racing fans' racing film. Forget melodramatic stories and corny dialogue and strap into a Gulf-Porsche 917K with McQueen for a true-to-life racing experience.

In truth, the film is incredibly short on story and very long on racing action. There is very little dialogue in the film at all and none in the opening 17 minutes.

The film, set against the 1971 race, focuses on Porsche team driver Michael Delaney (McQueen) returning to Le Mans one year after a

Steve McQueen stands between the Porsche 917K he drove in *Le Mans* and the Ford GT40 camera car. The helmeted camera man had control of several remote-control cameras mounted on the GT40. McQueen did all of his own driving in the movie. *Everett Collection*

vicious accident that put him out of the race and took the life of Ferrari driver Pierro Belgetti.

The main story is the race itself, and Delaney has his three-car team running at the front of the pack in a tight race with the three-car Ferrari 512LM team led by Delaney's nemesis, Erich Stahler (Siegfried Rauch). The subplot of Delaney's "relationship" with Belgetti's widow Lisa (Elsa Andersen) is told through their many awkward encounters at the track. Very few words are actually spoken between them as the two mostly exchange matching blue-eyed, stoic glares.

As day breaks on the rain-soaked event, Stahler spins his Ferrari, causing another of the Ferraris to crash heavily and fly off the track. The slow motion filming of the crash, the driver's escape, and the subsequent mushroom cloud explosion are a bit heavy-handed.

After the wreck Delaney loses concentration, nearly hitting a slower car. As a result, he writes off the Porsche in a big way. But Porsche team boss David Townsend (Leigh-Hunt) is quick to forgive Delaney and asks him to drive the final leg in the number 2 car to hold off Stahler and the Ferraris.

With time running out in the race, the lead Ferrari blows a tire, handing the lead to Delaney's teammate Larry Wilson (Christopher Waite). Delaney and Stahler duke it out in Wilson's rearview mirror as the checkered flag drops, followed by the two men exchanging nods in the pits.

The ending does not have you on the edge of your seat and the plot is someplace between thin and nonexistent, but this film has some of the best racing footage ever recorded. It also does an excellent job of capturing the feel of endurance racing.

Naturally, because it is a Steve McQueen film, there is a certain amount of controversy surrounding the making of *Le Mans*, mainly because the story and production were a mess from the start.

A promotional photo of McQueen and the Ferrari 512 driven by his nemesis played by Siegfried Rauch. Racing journalist Jabby Crombac was hired to faithfully re-create the pit scenes. Note McQueen is holding the wrong helmet. *Everett Collection*

The premise of the film came from McQueen himself, an accomplished racing driver, who had finished second at Sebring in a Porsche 908 in 1970. Originally he had proposed entering the Le Mans race with a camera on his car, but even after qualifying for the race the producers deemed it too risky.

Committed to a movie about the race, the track was rented for the weeks following the actual event. The weeks turned into three months because when filming began there was no script.

The concept was to film the race and then craft a movie around the real events. Filming began without a final script or screenplay even though an original script called *Le Mans* had been written three years earlier by Denne Bart Petitclerc. Petitclerc was brought on to punch up the script after watching the 1971 race.

McQueen insisted that the racing be as real as possible while the studio wanted a heavy story line. The result was a revolving door of script writers and automotive journalists brought in to take a stab at it. At one point the mercurial star proclaimed a script was not needed because it was all in his head. A final script was completed in late August after production had ceased for a month in mid-July.

In retrospect the racing action turned out to be the easiest thing to record. McQueen's Porsche 908 was entered in the 24-hour event with three cameras mounted on the car. It lasted the duration and recorded over 70,000 feet of film, only a fraction of which would make it into the film. Stationary cameras around the course logged another 50,000 feet while a flock of handheld cameras chalked up another 25,000.

After the Lola T70 IIIB dressed up as a Ferrari 512 was hurled into the woods for the accident scene, it laid untouched until the film could be processed to make sure the scene was captured on film. Once they knew the scene was recorded, the wreck was packed with explosives and detonated as the actor stumbled from the car.

Staging racing sequences to splice into the racing footage required exact replicas of the actual cars. A number of teams allowed the film crew to lease their cars after the race had been run. The rest of the cars were leased at a cost of $5,000 a week from racing driver Jo Siffert. The Swiss driver provided four Porsche 911s, two 914s, a Chevrolet Corvette, the 917Ks driven by McQueen, and his connections with Porsche also allowed for the Porsche 917LH "Longtail" to make a cameo appearance.

McQueen was adamant about the realism of the picture and demanded to do his own driving.

He also mandated that none of the Porsche drivers were allowed to have a blue helmet similar to his to prevent anyone from thinking there was a driving double.

Siegfried Rauch also did a fair amount of his own driving. Other drivers included Maston Gregory, Derek Bell, Richard Attwood, Jean-Pierre Jabouille, Brian Redman, Vic Elford, and Jo Siffert.

The car-to-car racing action was recorded from an open Ford GT40. Bob Slotemake drove the car while a cameraman ran a sophisticated 180-degree rotating Arriflex remote-control camera mounted on the rear deck. The actual racing cars also had intricate aluminum framing hanging off of their fronts, sides, and rears to deliver some of the exciting racing sequences and close-ups.

Despite McQueen's intense resolve for realism it would have been too much to ask that a Ferrari 512 and Porsche 917 be sacrificed in the name of art. Instead two tired Lola T70s were redressed with fiberglass bodywork to replicate the combatants. The cars had remote control systems installed to allow special effects man Malcolm King to drive the cars from atop a scaffold.

The Ferrari sequence ran amuck as the car got away from King on the first attempt and nearly took out the scaffold he was on. They got it right the second time as 10 cameras recorded the car rocketing up a disguised ramp and crashing through a Martini billboard.

The crash of the Porsche was rigged up in the same manner and went perfectly on the first attempt.

Production on the film dragged on for five months after the real race. Through it all the crew also had to continually re-create rain, fill the grandstands with 1,200 extras, pretend they were as warm as they would have been in June, and paint falling leaves green to match the grass. Thanks to a convoy of tanker trucks and massive sun shades they were able to pull it off. The staged sequences blend perfectly with the actual race footage.

Roll Call: Other Racing Films

The Racers (1955)
Great sports car racing footage from the mid-1950s including Kirk Douglas in a 1949 HVM. Dull story.

Viva Las Vegas (1964)
Elvis is a racer with some great sports racing cars set against Sinatra-era Vegas. This film features some of the greatest cars of the era—Cobra, Mercedes-Benz, Jaguar, Austin Healey, Ferrari—and some good racing action. Viva Ann Margaret.

Winning (1969)
Paul Newman races a variety of Fords and Can Am cars against Robert Wagner. *Winning* has a good story and some great vintage cars along with a view of Indy in the late 1960s.

On Any Sunday (1971)
The best documentary on off-road motorcycle racing produced to date.

Death Race 2000 (1975)
A bizarre combination of the Cannonball Run and hit-and-run as transcontinental racers earn points for speed and kills. Strange story but good stunts in cars created by Dean Jeffries.

Gumball Rally (1976)
The best of the Cannonball-Baker Trophy Dash take-offs, *Gumball* Rally features Michael Sarrazin in a Shelby Cobra and Raul Julia in a Ferrari leading the high-speed hi-jinx. Best line in a car movie? "What is behind me is not important," spoken by Raul Julia as he tossed the rearview mirror from the car.

Bobby Deerfield (1977)
This forgettable film casts Al Pacino as a Formula One driver. Actual, but sparse, race footage from 1977.

Greased Lightning (1977)
Richard Pryor stars as Wendell Scott, the first black driver to compete in Grand National Stock Car racing. A good story with authentic cars and some vintage racing footage.

King of the Mountain (1981)
This rarely seen movie has Harry Hamlin in a radically customized 1958 Porsche 356. He beats the clock and defeats a crazed Dennis Hopper in a tatty 1965 Corvette coupe on Mulholland Drive. Good cars, so-so story.

Black Moon Rising (1986)
Tommy Lee Jones in a saucer-shaped Bonneville Salt Flat car trying to outrun baddie Robert Vaughn.

Days of Thunder (1990)
Tom Cruise stars in formula plot that mirrors *Top Gun*. Cocksure driver wins then crashes and loses confidence. He then meets 25-year-old gorgeous brain surgeon (Nicole Kidman) and regains confidence to win the big race. Never came close to doing what *Grand Prix* did for Formula One.

CHAPTER 6

Flights of Fancy

In many of the chapters in this book the automobile or motorcycle is a prop. Not to slight the significance of each, because they are key elements of the stories, but they are there to lend credibility to the personalities, to complement the main characters. Why did David Janssen always have to take the bus on the TV series *Harry O*? Because his Austin-Healey was broken. The cars in this chapter, however, have personalities of their own and in some cases are the lead actors. They play the title role.

But these cars are not always the good guys. In movies like *Duel* (1971) and *The Car* (1977), cars and trucks are brought to life with nothing but evil-doing on their mechanical minds. They tenaciously pursue humans but never seem to need fuel. Steven King took it one step further in *Christine* (1983) and had the evil spirit of the car possess a young man while it ran down his enemies.

On the flip side, it is hard to believe that someone like Ian Fleming, who created a spy with a license to kill, could dream up the story of a loving car that flies. But he did, in *Chitty Chitty Bang Bang*. Similarly the Walt Disney folks brought a head-strong Volkswagen Beetle to life to help a down-on-his-luck racer win the trophy and the girl.

In each case there is just as much time spent on developing the character of the car as there is developing the characters of the human actors.

Chitty Chitty Bang Bang (1968)

MGM/United Artists
Director: Ken Hughes
Starring: Dick Van Dyke, Sally Ann Howes, Lionel Jeffries, and Benny Hill

Chitty Chitty Bang Bang was a children's fantasy from the pen of James Bond creator, Ian Fleming. He was something of a car buff and incorporated the name of an actual 1921 Brooklands mega-liter racing car into a fairy tale.

The story centers around a magical car restored by would-be inventor Caractacus Potts at the behest of his children. Once the car is road worthy it takes the Potts family on an amazing journey as they thwart the plans of the villainous Baron Bomburst of Vulgaria.

In 1968 a loose adaptation of the book was turned into a big-screen musical produced by Albert Broccoli (of James Bond fame) starring Dick Van Dyke. Clearly this was done in hopes of re-creating the Oscar-winning magic of *Mary Poppins* from four years earlier. The movie and the music were well wide of the Poppins mark, but time has been kind to the film and many of today's Baby Boomers have fond memories of the flick. Music and plot aside, Pinewood Studios and special effects director, John Stears (also from Bond), went to great lengths to create realistic effects for the 70-mm movie cameras.

The wicked Christine ready to kill. While the red-and-white two-tone is very striking, Furys were only offered in Buckskin Beige (off-white) in 1958. The blacked-out windows made it very easy to make the driverless sequences as the car exacts revenge. *Photofest*

Dick Van Dyke poses alongside *Chitty Chitty Bang Bang.* The car was built from an actual skiff and hand-formed sheet metal to replicate the look of a Bugatti. The assembly sat on a modified Ford ladder frame and was powered by a Ford V-6 engine and Borg-Warner automatic transmission. *Everett Collection*

One of the two cars created for *Chitty Chitty Bang Bang.* The car was 17 feet long from stem to stern and weighed in at almost 2 tons. In this scene, the car is photographed just prior to its transformation into a speedy boat. *Photofest*

This shot of *Chitty Chitty Bang Bang* really illustrates the 17-foot wheelbase of the custom-built car. A total of four cars were built, two with engines and two without. The metal body panels were fabricated from aluminum and the rear section was cut from an actual boat made of red and white cedar. *Photofest*

The scene where we first meet the lovable *Herbie* and before he earned his racing stripes and now famous number 53. A total of 26 Beetles were painted to match for the first film. Throughout the Herbie series the car always carried the California "black" license plate OFP 857. *Photofest*

The car itself was real, or at least the road car was real. It was built by production designer, Ken Adam, of Bond Aston Martin fame, along with Alan Mann, who prepped the Ford GT40s for racing at the 24 Hours of Le Mans.

They put Chitty on a customized Ford ladder frame that was lengthened at the front to house the leaf spring suspension. The exposed front suspension and spoke wheels authenticated the alleged prewar heritage of the car.

At least it looked vintage on the outside, because under the skin it was powered by an early Ford 3000 V-6 engine and a Borg-Warner semi-automatic transmission.

Obviously the engine did not come close to filling out the long hood, which was fabricated from aluminum and, along with the brass radiator

surround, was made to resemble Bugatti's infamous Royales. The boat-shaped body was an actual red-and-white cedar boat built by a Thames skiff builder. The aluminum dashboard and instruments were pirated from a World War I airplane, and the brasswork was salvaged from wrecked Edwardian Rolls-Royces.

When Chitty rolled onto the set she was 17 feet long and weighed in at 2 tons. Actually, two identical Chittys were built for the film so that no time would be lost in the event of an accident. Two mock-ups were also built without the drivetrains to be hung from a crane for the flying scene or to be mounted on power boats for the hovercraft scenes.

The two working cars exist today in England. One is in the Star Cars Museum in Kensington, and the other is in private hands and available for rent.

The Love Bug (1969)

Walt Disney Productions
Director: Robert Stevenson
Starring: Dean Jones, Michele Lee, Buddy Hackett,
David Tomlinson, and Joe Flynn

Herbie Rides Again (1974)

Walt Disney Productions
Director: Robert Stevenson
Starring: Helen Hayes, Ken Berry, Stefanie Powers,
and Keenan Wynn

Herbie Goes to Monte Carlo (1977)

Walt Disney Productions
Director: Vincent McEveety
Starring: Dean Jones, Don Knotts, Julie Sommars,
and Roy Kinnear

The indomitable spirit of the VW brought it great success in the choreographed racing scenes. To help the VW perform better, one of the cars received an engine and brakes from a Porsche 356. The car was never referred to as a Volkswagen throughout the film, and the logos were removed from the car. **Everett Collection**

In the climax of the film, owner Jim Douglas (Dean Jones) enters a rally to keep *Herbie* and win the girl (Michelle Lee). In scenes like this, and when the car does wheelies on the city streets, cables were hooked to the front and rear of the car to get it off the ground. *Everett Collection*

Herbie Goes Bananas (1980)

Walt Disney Productions
Director: Vincent McEveety
Starring: Charlie Martin Smith, Steven W. Burns, and Cloris Leachman

The original Volkswagen Beetle has been an icon ever since it was introduced to America in the 1950s. It was unlike anything else on the road at the time, and its unique looks and nickname of "Bug" gave it a real personality. What better car to bring to life in a fairy tale story and who better to do it than Walt Disney?

In March of 1969 *The Love Bug* was released in theaters. The picture was a loose adaptation of Gordon Buford's story entitled *Car-Boy-Girl*, originally published in 1956.

In Buford's book the VW was the real hero. Disney, however, was not completely sure about making the car the star even though the popularity of the number 53 Beetle eclipsed the human stars of the film. Herbie is the only character from the original film to be immortalized in the cement at Hollywood's infamous Grumman's Chinese Theater.

Leading the cast was Disney constant Dean Jones playing a down-on-his-luck racing driver, Jim Douglas. Douglas' career has fallen so low that he even gets bounced out of the local San Francisco demolition derby. Perhaps in 1969 it was believable that the City by the Bay hosted such events and that an unemployed race driver could afford Marina district housing.

The 1963 Sunroof Beetle lasted through four sequels. Here Herbie stars in Herbie Goes Bananas. *Photofest*

Nonetheless, after our hero is turtled in a demo derby and verbally run over by his agent, he is drawn into a new-car showroom. First he is drawn in by Michele Lee's legs, then by the Thorndyke Special perched on a rotating platform. The yellow Thorndyke Special was actually a Buick Apollo powered by the little aluminum 3.5-liter V8. To perpetuate the aura of speed and power, Jim Douglas describes the car as "Over 400 cubes, dual quads, all-synchro box, 0 to 60 in under 5."

During his visit he is befriended by the "little car" that mysteriously finds its way into the showroom and follows him home that night. It seems Douglas' roommate, Tennessee Steinmetz, played by an over-mugging Buddy Hackett, is the only one who realizes the car has a mind of its own. He also names the car "Herbie" after his uncle.

Douglas spends the rest of the film spanking the competition in every race he and *Herbie* enter, thanks to the indomitable spirit of the car. In the end he beats all odds, defeats the conniving Thorndyke, and wins the love of the woman.

Forgetting the fact that nearly all of the race scenes were choreographed and sped up, this is a fine family film with the predictable Disney plot and great shots of Laguna Seca and Willow Springs, and a de Milleian cast of 1960s sports racers.

For the record, *Herbie* is a white 1963 sunroof Beetle, according to Walt Disney Studios. However, at the start Disney was not sold on the idea of using a VW in the movie, despite the fact that Buford used one in the book, so they held a casting call of sorts at the employee entrance to the studio. A row of cars was parked inside the gate, and the production crew watched for reactions as people passed by. When they saw how the Bug was received, they knew they had their star.

Prior to Disney closing their archives it was published that 26 VW Beetles were painted for the part of *Herbie*. But there are many unconfirmed reports that as many as 40 different cars were used. While the paint on all the cars matched, they were not all identical, and if you know your Bugs well you can spot the different cars used in the film. Disney even used an oval-window car!

The number 53 was selected by Bill Walsh, who wrote the screenplay from the book. He is said to have chosen the number because he "was seeing a lot of 53s at the time," including major league baseball pitcher Don Drysdale's number.

Two of Disney's most lovable stars, *Herbie* and Helen Hayes. Because *The Love Bug* was such a box office success, Volkswagen participated in the launch of the sequel, Herbie Rides Again, including 300,000 posters for dealers to distribute and a factory decal package. *Photofest*

The interior of each car was painted gray to help hide reflections from studio lights during the filming.

It is clear Disney was still not 100 percent behind the car since the VW logos on the front and rear are blanked out and the VW hubcaps were replaced with smooth "baby moons." Neither the names *Volkswagen* nor *Beetle* were used in the film, and occasionally the word "bug" was used prominently but not to refer to the car. It was simply know as the "little car."

Obviously the factory-built little car and its stock 1,200-cc engine and its 40 horsepower would not be very convincing in the racing scenes or when Herbie had to show some pep. Several cars were fitted with a VW Bus engine that put out 65 horsepower to make things more realistic.

The car for the racing scenes received a Porsche 356 engine that produced 90 horsepower and could make a valiant effort at keeping up with the Corvette, Cobras, and Jaguars on the track. In addition, the car also got the 356's brakes, camber compensators, sway bars, and Koni shocks. The car was said to be capable of 115 miles per hour, but we all know that is still not enough power to do a wheelie. The wheelies were achieved with cables, as was the scene where *Herbie* skips across the water.

Throughout the film *Herbie* made his way around town without a driver. In reality the car had a backseat driver. A second steering column was mounted in the rear seat of the car and connected to the main steering column with a chain and sprockets. The pedals were moved back to allow the driver complete control.

On one stunt car the body was mounted backwards on the chassis to allow *Herbie* to drive backwards more easily.

The Love Bug was the top-grossing film of 1969 and spawned three sequels and a short-lived 1982 television series.

The unforgettable opening sequence as *Christine* is born. A furniture factory was converted to look like a 1957 Chrysler assembly line. Industry executives toured the movie location and were impressed with the authenticity. *Photofest*

Herbie Rides Again was released in the summer of 1974 with a media blitz and total cooperation with Volkswagen. Some 300,000 *Herbie* posters were sent to dealers and every dealer had a Herbie replica on the showroom floor. *Herbie* decal kits were also available at VW parts counters.

Herbie's appearance changed slightly in the new film. A spotlight was mounted on the hood, and the blue stripe was made darker.

Three years later, in June of 1977, Disney released *Herbie Goes to Monte Carlo. Herbie* shed his spotlight and also became the first and only car in history to be issued a bonafide U.S. passport. Since it is illegal to forge a passport, Disney got special dispensation from the U.S. government to issue an actual passport. The document states Herbie is 5 feet tall and lists "sunroof" instead of hair and "sealed-beam" for eye color.

Herbie Goes Bananas was released in the summer of 1980. By this time the theme had worn out its welcome and lost its star power. The *Herbie* franchise had run out of gas. The only redeeming qualities about the last films were the great cars and race tracks that jumped out from all the silliness and sappiness.

Dean Jones reprised his role as Jim Douglas in a short-lived TV show called *Herbie the Love Bug*, which aired on CBS in March and April of 1982.

Today there are countless Herbie replicas on the streets. It is not known where all of the cars went, but several are documented to be in the hands of private collector's.

Christine (1983)

Columbia Pictures
Director: John Carpenter
Starring: Keith Gordon, John Stockwell, Alexandra Paul, Robert Prosky, and Harry Dean Stanton

Horror films go in and out of fashion. Just when you think there are no more slasher films to be had, a spate of them flood your local theaters.

Back in the 1980s it wasn't just any scary movie flooding the theaters. Each year brought us the latest cinematic interpretation of a different bestseller from the prolific Stephen King. *Christine* was brought to us in 1983, and if ever there was a matched set of novelist and director to bring a story to life, it was King and *Christine* director John Carpenter. The latter is as prolific at scary celluloid as the former is at spine-tingling print.

The film follows the book pretty well, at least in comparison to other King books turned into films. *Christine* is the story of Arnie Cunningham (Keith Gordon), the poster-child for high school nerds. He gets beat up for his lunch money every day, and his only friend is Dennis Guilder (John Stockwell), a jock who defends Arnie when he can.

As the two boys are driving home from school, Arnie spies the decaying remains of a 1958 Plymouth Fury with a for-sale sign in the window. The owner is a creepy old coot who looks as bad as the car. He tells the lads about *Christine* and her nefarious past, which includes killing his brother and niece. Dead brother or no, Arnie must have *Christine*. Against Dennis' pleading, Arnie buys the car and vows to restore it.

Arnie does little actual work as the possessed car restores itself through Arnie's affection while its innate evil takes possession of Arnie.

Before you know it the zits are gone, he no longer needs glasses, he's one of the best dressers in school, and he's dating the hottest girl in the student body (Alexandra Paul).

Christine's power soon has Arnie too big for his britches, and anyone who crosses him is stalked and killed by the Fury in some violent special effects. The cop (Harry Dean Stanton) suspects Arnie, but his girlfriend and best friend know the car is the real culprit. As the duo attempt to exorcise Arnie from *Christine*, both the car and the boy perish.

Anyone who knows anything about 1950s Plymouths is aware that both the film and book are rife with flaws. The murderous *Christine* is described in the book as a four-door, even though '58 Furys were only available as two-doors. In the opening of the film we see *Christine* being built on a faithfully re-created plant assembly line

The bad guys take out their frustrations on the freshly restored Fury. To simulate the car restoring itself, electric servos were mounted under the bodywork with arms attached to the body panels. As the arms pulled inward the car would become dented. The film was then run in reverse. *Columbia Pictures Industries*

Aside from the 16 Furys, Savoys, and Belvederes that were destroyed to make *Christine*, a 1968 Chevrolet Camaro was also wrecked in the explosive gas station sequence. A faux station was built and blown up for the effect. *Columbia Pictures Industries*

staged in a furniture plant. When *Christine* is born, she is red, but 1958 Furys were offered only in Buckskin Beige.

On the flip-side you can see the logic used to create the story. Fury is far more sinister than Savoy, and beige is not a terribly menacing color.

For many car buffs the real flaw in this film was the destruction of so many cars. Reports in-

dicate that somewhere between 13 and 16 cars were destroyed while making the movie.

Film production began with Columbia Pictures hunting down cars for the film, scouring junkyards, and contacting Plymouth owners located through the California Department of Motor Vehicles. Because actual Furys were scarce, several Belvedere and Savoy hardtops were painted to

The death of *Christine* as the bulldozer squashes the evil out of the car. *Photofest*

Doctor Brown (Christopher Lloyd) and the time-traveling DeLorean. Three cars were purchased and built by the studio for a total of $150,000. *Photofest*

look the part. The studio reportedly budgeted $10,000 per vehicle for the restoration and eventual destruction of each car.

The incredible special effects of the car restoring itself were achieved by mounting hydraulic motors inside the bodywork with arms attached to the body panels. The motors pulled the panels inwards, creating the creases and dents. The film was then run in reverse to give the effect.

The gas station scene was achieved through the re-creation of an entire service station in remote California. The entire thing was then blown up in one take. And yes, a real 1968 Camaro was also destroyed in the scene.

None of the cars used in the film were saved or were even capable of being saved. The film did bring out a number of *Christine* replicas on the car show circuit. A bitter pill for most Plymouth aficionados.

Back to the Future (1985)
Universal Pictures
Director: Robert Zemeckis
Starring: Michael J. Fox, Christopher Lloyd, Crispin Glover, Lea Thompson, and Marc McClure

"You made a time machine—out of a DeLorean?!" exclaims an incredulous Marty McFly (Michael J. Fox) to Doctor Emmett Brown (Christopher Lloyd). The doctor replies that if you are going to travel through time, why not do it with some style. The stainless-steel bodywork also helped flux dispersal, which was critical for time travel.

Very few carmakers get this big of a plug in a movie, even when it is all in fun and the car is customized. But *Back to the Future* introduced the stainless-steel exotic to a bigger audience than the nightly news did during John DeLorean's much-publicized fall from grace. Of course it was not enough to save the man or the company, but it did make the car a household name.

The DeLorean itself was the catalyst for the comic story of a 1980s teenager (Fox) who accidentally travels back in time to the mid-1950s. Once back in the 1950s he has to unite his virtually incompatible parents in order to prevent his own existence from being erased. At the same time he has to figure out how to recharge the DeLorean and return to his rightful place in history. A very entertaining story produced by Steven Speilberg's production company, Amblin Entertainment, and Universal, and directed by Robert Zemeckis.

The DeLorean was chosen as homage to the spaceship drawings from the 1950s because of the stainless-steel body and gullwing doors. Here Michael J. Fox has just traveled to the 1950s. *Photofest*

This film was followed by two sequels that, while clever, lacked the punch of the first. The De-Lorean was featured throughout the series of films.

The time machine in the original script was a contraption that occupied an entire room. Writer/producer Bob Gale and Zemeckis toyed with the Star Trek theme of molecular assembly and reassembly but decided to make the time machine mobile.

They quickly decided on the DeLorean because of its stainless-steel body and gullwing doors. In a way it looked like a 1950s drawing of a spaceship.

Since the "Doc" was an absent-minded sort, they knew the car couldn't be too slick and polished. Studio artist Ron Cobb was charged with coming up with an illustration of a car that looked homemade. Production illustrator Andy Probert enhanced the blueprints.

Once the look was finalized the transportation crew was sent out to purchase three DeLoreans. After canvassing the classifieds, three cars were bought for a total of $50,000. To keep costs down and further enhance the look of the car, only real spare parts were used and very little was made from scratch.

Kevin Pike at Filmtrix Inc. removed the rear window and louvers and built a small nuclear reactor on top of the engine bay. A variety of tubing, housings, coils, generators, vents, and even a Dodge Polara hubcap were sourced and assembled on the engine's heat shield.

The interior of the car was jammed full of gauges, wires, and digital read-outs to further the

Mad Max drove an AMC AMX with a supercharger in the futuristic world of scarce gasoline. *Photofest*

homemade appearance. Of course the critical time clocks were prominently mounted on the center console.

According to Dr. Brown, the time machine was electrical, requiring just a small nuclear kick to generate the necessary 1.21 jigawatts that made it work. The stunt DeLorean in fact had extensive electrical enhancements to help create the time-travel illusion, though none of the additional components required uranium for fuel.

Neon tubing was attached to the underside of the vehicle, and three 100-amp car batteries were wired in parallel to boost amperage. Two inverters converted DC to AC and lit the neon as the car reached the critical 88 miles per hour.

A special effects man riding in the car also had control of high-voltage igniters that lit fire-jets mounted at each wheel. This further enhanced the explosive charge of time travel. The re-entry effect was enhanced with a CO_2 extinguisher in the cockpit that actually vented

through the nuclear steam vents on the rear deck.

Two identical running models were built while a third was kept in a state of disassembly for close-ups and as a parts car for the other two. The studio spent a total of $150,000 building the time-traveling DeLoreans.

Roll Call: Other Flights of Fancy

The Absent-Minded Professor (1961)
Fred MacMurray makes a flying Ford Model T phaeton.
It's a Mad, Mad, Mad, Mad World (1963)
A zany chase as the greatest comedians of the day look for dough left by Jimmy Durante. Nonstop, hilarious action. "Stop kiddin', will ya? Just press the button marked booze."

The Yellow Rolls-Royce (1965)
The experiences of a variety of people who own the same late 1930s Rolls.

The Ecto 1 was built from a 1959 Cadillac ambulance. *Photofest*

Duel (1972)
A Plymouth Valiant performs valiantly as Dennis Weaver outruns evil semi-truck. Steven Spielberg's first feature film.

The Car (1977)
A late-night cable TV staple that quickly puts you to sleep. Possessed, driverless Lincoln Mark III on steroids kills people until James Brolin buries it in the desert. Barris built the car to spec, and Brolin deserves award for playing along.

Mad Max (1979)
The first in a trio of films starring Mel Gibson as a brooding highway cop in futuristic, post-apocalyptic Australia. Radical custom "vehicles" compete to the death for fuel.

Ghostbusters (1984)
George Barris added cartoon-like elements to a 1959 Cadillac ambulance to make "Ecto 1" for the boys to drive.

Ferris Bueller's Day Off (1986)
Smug but loveable Matthew Broderick skips school in a Ferrari 250GT Spyder California.

Planes, Trains & Automobiles (1987)
Hilarious Steve Martin and John Candy film. None of the auto manufacturers wanted to provide a car after reading the script. Can you blame them? The Chrysler K-car was cast perfectly.

National Lampoon's Vacation (1983)
Great parody of the American ritual of the family vacation on the road starring Chevy Chase. Even the traditional station wagon is roasted in the form of the Family Truckster in Metallic Pea with the optional Rallye Fun-Pack.

CHAPTER 7

TV Cars and Bikes

When Adam West was persuaded to don tights and a cape for the campy prime-time series *Batman* in 1966, no one really knew what was going to happen. *Batman's* incredible but short-lived popularity led to a cult following for the show that lives on today. More important, it created a rolling icon: the *Batmobile*.

With minimal resources available, thanks to a tight studio budget, George Barris created the car from the 1955 Lincoln Futura show car in a scant few weeks. If you have ever seen the show car, you know that Mr. Barris did not add much to it other than the jet-black paint, mag wheels, bolt-on bogus gadgets, and a few bat symbols. Yet, the enormous popularity of the car primed the pump for countless television cars to become as famous as their human costars.

Hot on the heels of the Batmobile, Dean Jeffries was contracted to build the *Black Beauty* from a common Chrysler. This car was an aid the *Green Hornet* in his fight against organized crime. Two years later, Jeffires created the *Monkeemobile* from a Pontiac GTO for the Fabricated Four.

The phenomenon of automotive stars stealing the thunder of their human costars goes beyond the custom car craze of the 1960s. Would anyone have appreciated brass-era cars (or even known what a Porter was) if Jerry Van Dyke had not talked to the four-wheeled incarnation of his mother? Peter Falk made Peugeot a recognized, albeit tatty, name in *Columbo* and a Ferrari Daytona Spyder kit-car enhanced Don Johnson's swagger in *Miami Vice*.

These are the cars that have risen to the level of stars. Today many of these vehicles are more memorable than the shows they were in or the actors who drove them.

The Green Hornet (1966–1967 [ABC])

20th Century Fox Television/Greenway Productions
Starring: Van Williams, Bruce Lee, Wende Wagner, Lloyd Gough, and Walter Brooke

Anxious to capitalize on the instant and smashing success of the prime-time Batman series, ABC turned the same crew loose on another campy crime-fighter drama.

The *Green Hornet* debuted on September 9, 1966, with Van Williams in the title role and martial arts legend Bruce Lee as Kato. The show was an update of the popular radio serial from the 1930s and 1940s with some necessary updates. In the original radio series the Green Hornet was the grandnephew of the Lone Ranger, one of America's earliest masked crime fighters.

The updated *Green Hornet* TV plot was very similar to the *Batman* TV plot, with Williams playing the dual role of the Green Hornet and alter ego Britt Reid. As the millionaire-playboy and owner-publisher of the *Daily Sentinel* newspaper, Reid would crusade against evil-doers in his green mask with matching green fedora and green topcoat. Under the topcoat was a suit with a white shirt and tie easily promoting him to one of the most dapper crime-fighters in history.

Don Johnson and the famously faked 1971 Plymouth 'Cuda 426 Hemi convertible. *Everett Collection*

Black Beauty, the automotive star of *The Green Hornet,* and her costars Van Williams and Bruce Lee. Dean Jeffries removed the Chrysler New Yorker bumper and restyled the grille with revolving headlamps and hidden doors that opened to fire missiles. The green lenses were for night driving with white lenses for daylight. The missiles were actually hobby-store rockets. Electric motors opened and closed the doors operated from inside the car.

Unlike the cartoonish villains in *Batman*, the Green Hornet thwarted more conventional baddies including the very topical organized crime. He was also far more mysterious than Batman, working almost exclusively under the cover of darkness and usually only seen by the bad guys. To help secure his secrecy the Green Hornet was listed as a wanted criminal by the police.

Britt Reid's dual identity was known only to his manservant and partner Kato (Lee), his secretary Casey Case (Wende Wagner), and District Attorney Scanlon (Walter Brooke). Like Batman, and Superman for that matter, no one was ever able to make the connection between the popular Reid and the secretive Green Hornet.

Each installment opened with a dark screen as trumpet master Al Hirt played a frenetic arrangement of Rimsky Korsakov's "Flight of the Bumble Bee". Suddenly the Green Hornet yells, "Faster Kato!" followed by screeching tires. Then the opening credits roll while a voice-over by the unmistakable voice of Gary Owens says "Another challenge for the Green Hornet, his aid Kato, and their rolling arsenal the *Black Beauty*. On police records a wanted criminal, Green Hornet is really Britt Reid, owner-publisher of the *Daily Sentinel*, his duel identity known only to his secretary and the district attorney. And now, to

Black Beauty in action, taken in a rare daytime photo. The Green Hornet operated under the cover of darkness, so the car was mostly seen on television at night. Jeffries attributes the filming of the black car in the dark as the reason the car never caught on like the Batmobile. **Photofest**

protect the rights and lives of decent citizens, rides THE GREEN HORNET."

The tire sounds emanated from the Green Hornet's rolling arsenal known as *Black Beauty*. Named for its wet licorice black paint and stylish good looks, it was a one-of-a-kind anti-crime supercar designed and built by the star Britt Reid.

The car was chauffeur driven by Kato with the Green Hornet riding in the rear. On the back of Kato's bench seat was a control panel ala James Bond with an incredible array of offensive and defensive weapons and gadgets. At the Green Hornet's disposal were front and rear missiles, front and rear flame-throwers, rear oil slick and smoke-screen, and a closed circuit flying spy satellite.

There was also a closet on the back of the seat for the Green Hornet's disguise and a compartment in the rear pillar for his various nonlethal gas guns and metal-penetrating sting guns.

Up front there was a telephone in the dashboard and a secret compartment for Kato's throwing knives.

The actual car used in the series was built from a 1966 Chrysler Imperial by Hollywood customizer Dean Jeffries. Jeffries was selected for the job because he was well known around the Fox Studios and had originally been contracted to build the TV *Batmobile*. According to Jeffries the whole comic book superhero thing was hot in

The Green Hornet and Kato ready for action. This shows good detail of the extended rear pillar, fender skirts, and lack of door handles. Jeffries had a very short time to convert the New Yorker to a stealth car, so many of the changes were quick but stylish cosmetic elements.

This interior view of *Black Beauty* reveals some of the special equipment used by the Green Hornet to catch the bad guys. Among other things, the car's dashboard contained a telephone and a special compartment for Kato's throwing knives.

Dean Jeffries poses with the *Monkeemobile* near his shop in the Hollywood hills shortly after completing construction. The car is based on a 1966 Pontiac GTO convertible with the tri-carb 389 V-8. Jeffries lengthened the nose and rear panels to give the illusion of a much bigger car; however, the wheelbase was not modified. *Dean Jeffries*

the mid-1960s, and the studio had been talking about a host of potential projects. The first was *The Green Hornet*.

The Imperial was selected because Chrysler had been working with the production studio and wanted to be involved in the project. Jeffries was given the car with minimal time and minimal instruction, other than that they wanted the car full of gizmos and they wanted it quickly.

First Jeffries removed the front bumper and cut off the nose of the car. He lengthened it slightly and completely reshaped it with a protruding chrome grille in the center flanked by revolving headlights and hidden lower missile doors.

The headlights flipped over from conventional white lights to dual-beam green lights for night vision. Flush-fitting doors that dropped down to reveal eight missiles on each side ran along the lower part of the fascia. The doors had to be made of thin metal to operate smoothly and fit flush when closed. Jeffries sourced the rockets at a local hobby store and mounted them onto the assembly to give the illusion of protruding when the doors opened.

A small door at the bottom center of the grille opened to reveal a flame-thrower nozzle.

Switches in the car actuated all of these features, which were driven by small electric motors mounted between the shroud and the nose.

At the back of the car Jeffries removed the bumper and resculpted the entire rear of the car. The bumper was redone to fit more flushly into the car. Missile doors similar to those at the front were installed in the lower valance panel, complete with hobby-shop rockets.

The centrally located rear gas cap and filler neck were removed and replaced with a fuel cell mounted near the differential. The gas cap was replaced with a flush-mounted disk that would drop down electrically, giving way to the grease-gun-flame-thrower assembly. The flame thrower was connected to a small butane tank in the trunk. When the flame effect was needed, the butane valve was opened and the nozzle lit with a pocket lighter. The rest of the trunk was filled with electric motors to run the various effects and house the flying spy satellite.

To produce the effect, Jeffries cut a hole in the center of the trunk lid and made small dual doors that opened outward. As the doors opened, they pulled the satellite device upward to make it look like it was about to be launched.

Thin vertical taillights were recessed into the trunk lid, draping from the top of the lid down to the rear bumper. Jeffries was not completely happy with the way they looked, but he said it was all he could think of at the time.

The original look of the Chrysler was further disguised by extending the roofline at the rear. Fiberglass panels were added to extend and square off the top, creating a very wide C-pillar that was covered in the same black padding as the rest of the top.

That was the only fiberglass used in the customization of the car. Jeffries believed in working with metal. Even the redesigned rear bumper took two men to lift.

Finally Jeffries put new wheels on the car and created rear fender skirts to round out the more formal appearance of the car. Hidden behind the rear wheels were brushes that dropped down to erase *Black Beauty's* tire tracks.

One other element critical to the anonymity of the hero and his car was short metal bars that extended approximately 12 inches longitudinally from all four corners of the car. These were extended when the car returned to Britt Reid's garage where arms would clamp onto each one and the floor would revolve, hiding the *Beauty* upside down under the floor and returning Reid's Chrysler convertible.

Many of the features built into the car were never seen on television, including the phone, the secret compartments in the rear passenger area, and a desklike assembly that flipped out of the rear armrest.

The rest of the car was completely straight and stock just as Jeffries had received it.

Unfortunately the show and the car never caught on like the *Batmobile*. Jeffries speculates the reason may be that all the shots featuring the car were done at night and a black car in the dark doesn't look like much.

After the show was cancelled the original *Black Beauty* was left on a Fox lot for approximately a year until it was purchased by a Fox employee. He used it to cruise the Hollywood hot rod boulevard scene for a while but received several tickets for not having proper safety equipment. So he added mirrors and a real bumper and welded the missile doors shut to become street legal.

After doing all of that, he set out to restore the car properly and stripped everything off the car. Simultaneously his career took off and the car languished in the elements for more than 15 years.

In a chance meeting in 1990 an enthusiast named J. R. Goodman bought the car with the sole purpose of returning *Black Beauty* to her original glory. The only way to get the job done right was to return the car to her creator. Dean Jeffries spent over a year lovingly restoring the car to better-than-original appearance, and he even tried to buy the car back several times.

Goodman showed *Black Beauty* for a few years before selling the car to a private collector in the greater Los Angeles area where she sits today.

The Monkees (1966–1968 (NBC))

NBC, Raybert Productions, Screen Gems Television
Starring: Davy Jones, Peter Tork, Micky Dolenz, Michael Nesmith
Musical advisor: Don Kirshner

In September of 1966 NBC debuted a half-hour situation comedy that was a direct rip-off of the real-life Beatles and their hit 1964 film *A Hard Days Night*. As was the movie, the show was irreverent, unconventional, and completely 1960s.

Each week the show followed the madcap misadventures of Peter, Davy, Micky, and Mike, four band mates and housemates who would get into ridiculous situations as

The MPC model kit that was the basis for the creation of the car. Over seven million *Monkeemobile* models were sold by MPC. While the model company was thrilled with the result, Pontiac was unhappy with the radically customized car. *Jim Wangers*

WIN A GUEST ROLE
on "THE MONKEES" TV SHOW
and this customized PONTIAC GTO!

©1967, Raybert Productions, inc.

Kellogg's
TV Screen-Stakes

1,516 PRIZES GIVEN AWAY!

- **GRAND PRIZE**—All-expense-paid, 7-day trip to Hollywood to appear on "The Monkees" NBC-TV show, plus a 1968 Pontiac GTO Convertible*. This customized GTO has a 360 H.P. engine, 4-speed transmission with Hurst shifter, rally gauge instruments, tachometer, and other exciting sports car features.

- *15 MORE BIG PRIZES OF PONTIAC GTO HARDTOPS*—each with all the great sports car features described above for the GTO Convertible.

- *1,500 CONSOLATION PRIZES*—
    "Monkees" LP Albums.

*If winner of one of the Pontiac GTO prizes is a minor, Kellogg's reserves the right to award car to winner's parent or guardian.

Be a winner...nothing to buy ...easy to enter!

Picture yourself winning a guest role on one of "The Monkees" NBC-TV shows, and this fabulous new Pontiac GTO Convertible. Or, maybe you'll win one of the GTO Hardtop or "Monkees" Record Album prizes. You have 1,516 chances to win! Enter often—the more you enter, the better your chances are! Don't wait—all "TV Screen-stakes" entries must be postmarked before May 5, 1968.

GET DETAILS ON SPECIAL KELLOGG'S® RICE KRISPIES® AND RAISIN BRAN® PACKAGES, OR ON FREE STORE ENTRY FORMS AT YOUR GROCER'S!

"Screen-stakes" void in Wisconsin and wherever else prohibited by law.

©1968 by Kellogg Company

GET "AUTOGRAPHED" PICTURES OF "THE MONKEES" ON SPECIAL KELLOGG'S PUFFA PUFFA RICE AND OKs® PACKAGES, TOO!

they tried to survive in the Los Angeles rock-'n'-roll scene.

Despite all the silliness, the show proved to be groundbreaking television. All kinds of unconventional film techniques were used to achieve a staccato and frenetic pace that had never been done on any program prior to that time. In hindsight it could be called MTV 15 years ahead of its time.

To ensure the Monkees concept followed the Beatles mold (right down to making the name a play on words), the band members had to be actors first and "musicians" second. NBC chose the four players from a casting call that drew over 500 applicants. The foursome had little musical experience, but they could and did sing the songs written for them by the hit-maker duo of Tommy Boyce and Bobby Hart.

Several of the Boyce-Hart penned songs became unexpected, bona fide chart busters. In fact, their first single, "Last Train to Clarksville," hit number 1 on the Billboard charts just weeks before the first episode aired, which was like pre-ignition to the impending Monkees' explosion.

Equally unexpected was the conception and birth of a Monkee-themed car. The *Monkeemobile* became infamous the first day it rolled from creator Dean Jeffries shop and quickly became a 1960s hot rod icon in its own right.

Despite being designed and named for the show, the *Monkeemobile* was actually quite separate from the series and especially the band itself. That is partly because of how the car came about and the politically charged firestorm in Detroit when the project was completed.

The entire concept of a *Monkeemobile* was the brainchild of George Toteff, then president and CEO of Model Productions Corporation, better known as MPC. Toteff was looking for a customized car to tie in with the show that he could make and sell as a plastic model kit. At the time he was working with Dean Jeffries, one of Hollywood's hottest young customizers. Coincidentally, Jeffries was also under contract with Universal Studios which was producing the Monkees show. As the key players came together, Toteff contacted his friend Jim Wangers who was handling Pontiac's public relations and advertising at the McManus, John & Adams agency.

Wangers quickly recognized it as a huge promotional opportunity and promptly persuaded Pontiac to furnish two red 1966 GTO convertibles for Jeffries to work his magic. The original cars had tri-carb 389-ci V-8 engines, four-speed transmissions, and 3:55 "Safe-T-track" rear ends.

Everything about the building of the *Monkeemobile* was rushed and tangled. MPC wanted a radical looking car that would sell model kits while Pontiac wanted a recognizable and promotable GTO-based TV star. Jeffries could not serve two masters; he sided with the studio since they were paying the bills.

In just one month, Jeffries delivered a highly modified version of the original car that screamed 1960s Hollywood custom. On first glance you could barely recognize the GTO roots of his creation, but the longer you looked at it, the more it did look like a GTO. The genius of Jeffries work was in the simplicity of how he created the car.

The original grille assembly and entire rear fascia were removed, and the nose and tail were elongated with basic sheet metal formed to match the existing panels. The Pontiac split grille became an exaggerated and severely raked snout that was almost shark-like in appearance.

The hood was cut and dished with a hole in the center to give way to the chrome-plated Art Chrisman 6-71 supercharger mounted atop the engine. To channel this power and make it easier to do wheelies, the rear axle was solidly mounted and additional weights were put in the back of the car.

The factory windshield was cut off and tilted up, and a chrome piece was glued to the center to give the illusion of a taller split windshield.

Jeffries lengthened the aft portion of the front wheelwells to allow the functional chrome exhaust trumpets to escape. He also rigged a tamer exhaust that exited just ahead of the rear wheels.

The rear end got exaggerated taillights, complete with a dragsteresque parachute and quick-fill gas cap on top of the now-very-short rear deck. Jeffries removed the trunk area and gas

In 1968, Pontiac partnered with Kelloggs to promote the new GTO. As a part of the "TV Screen Stakes," winners could receive a walk-on part on *The Monkees* and win a new GTO convertible. The *Monkeemobile* and the GTO were seen on more than 40 million cereal boxes. *Jim Wangers*

The Monkees—Michael Nesmith, Peter Tork, Micky Dolenz, and Davy Jones,—and the *Monkeemobile. Marty Eck*

tank to install a third row of seats so that there were two rows of bucket seats and a bench at the rear. A small racing fuel cell was located beneath the rear seat.

The rear wheel arches received 4-inch fender flares and the original wheel and tire package was replaced with Ansen mags and Formula One Super Stock rubber.

A permanent hardtop was built to resemble a convertible top and covered in tan orlon to match the tan vinyl upholstery. Two people could unbolt the top and lift it off the car.

The rest of the car is pure GTO as it was built in the factory. There have been many suggestions that the wheelbase was altered because of the illusion Jeffries created by changing the sheet metal at each end. The real craftsmanship in the car is exemplified in Jeffries' work and the fact that the car is all pounded and formed metal. No fiberglass was used.

Jeffries' crew worked around the clock to produce identical cars in one month. Unfortunately, Wangers and his chief client, Pontiac's general manager, John DeLorean, were not happy with the end result. They felt the car was far more radical than they had in mind and not at all recognizable as a GTO. There was no time left to start over or make changes, so the GTO logos were put back on the car and it went out as Jeffries had created it.

MPC, on the other hand, was thrilled with Jeffries' results because it provided the perfect style to base a kit on. MPC sold over 7 million *Monkeemobile* model kits, second in company history to The Dukes of Hazzard's *General Lee*.

According to Jeffries, when the car was delivered to the studio the "kids," went for a joyride in the car and tore it up. The output was simply far too much to handle. To make the car more tractable a dummy supercharger was mounted over a regular four-barrel carburetor, and the weights were removed from the rear.

Although the car was only seen in a handful of episodes and the opening credits from the second season, the *Monkeemobile* became an icon for the band and the era. Car enthusiasts would watch each week just to catch a glimpse of the car. Meanwhile Wangers was tuning in in hopes of not seeing the car and would breathe a sigh of relief when the credits rolled. According to Wangers the studio was told to use the car sparingly.

Despite the popularity of the car among enthusiasts and model-builders, the Pontiac-Monkees tie had become known as the "Wangers debacle" at General Motors' headquarters even a year later. However, that opinion changed quickly when Wangers hooked up with Kelloggs in a blockbuster promotion.

The cereal giant launched the "TV Screen Stakes" on the back of their most popular cereal boxes in 1968. The grand prize was a guest appearance on the Monkees TV show and a new 1968 Pontiac GTO convertible. There were 15 second prizes of a GTO hardtop, and 1,500 third-prize winners were awarded a Monkees album. The *Monkeemobile* and the GTO appeared on more than 42 million Rice Krispies and Raisin Bran boxes. The promotion was a smashing success and Wangers was back in the good graces of Pontiac.

Some 35 years later the *Monkeemobile* is still popular. Original MPC kits and Corgi toys fetch hundreds of dollars in the collector markets. And both of the original cars still exist.

The number two car is owned by the famous George Barris and is on display in his Gatlinberg, Tennessee, museum.

Jeffries' first creation, the number one car, is in the hands of a private collector in New York state. How the car got there is quite an amazing story.

After the TV series was done the car remained on tour with the band for a short time. Its last known whereabouts was Australia, from the group's last international tour. Unfortunately, the car was left behind.

For several years Jeffries tried to reclaim the car, but extradition proved too difficult and the car slipped from sight.

The *Monkeemobile* resurfaced in Puerto Rico at a government foreclosure auction where a private collector picked it up for $5,000.

The car turned out to be in relatively good shape, needing only minimal restoration. Today the car turns up at shows, primarily in the eastern United States and sometimes at national Pontiac events.

Then Came Bronson (1969–1970(NBC))
MGM Television
Starring: Michael Parks

Believe it or not the premiere of the short-lived series *Then Came Bronson* was not a knee-jerk reaction to the 1969 box office success of *Easy Rider*. The pilot TV movie for the series was already in the can when the Peter Fonda–Dennis Hopper period classic began making box office history in the theater.

The pilot episode and the title for the show were fashioned around veteran actor Charles Bronson, who was originally pegged for the lead. Unfortunately, Bronson declined the role and Michael Parks was chosen for the main character, yet the original title remained.

Parks played Jim Bronson, a city newspaper reporter searching for the meaning of life after the suicide of his best friend. He quits his job, sells all his possessions (with the exception of a sleeping bag, leather jacket, Ray Bans, and a knit cap), and rides across America on his late friend's Harley-Davidson Sportster. Each week Bronson's search takes him to new towns where he meets new people and takes odd jobs to support himself.

While the bike in the show was clearly recognizable as an 883 Sportster, all of the Harley-Davidson logos were removed. The "peanut" gas tank was painted red with a triangular decal on each side depicting an eye similar to the top of the pyramid on the back of the dollar bill.

According to an MGM press release, the Bronson bike also had a chromed and bobbed front fender, bobbed rear fender, a 21-inch aluminum front wheel, custom leather seat, custom sport headlight, and chrome-plated chain guard and voltage regulator.

Harley-Davidson supplied the motorcycles for the pilot and the show. A total of three Sportsters were used for production along with a Harley-Davidson Sprint 350, a Harley-Davidson Rapido 125, and a Czechoslovakian CZ. One of the Sportsters was not used on-screen because it

Michael Parks gets ready for his *Then Came Bronson* close-up aboard his 1969 Harley-Davidson 883 Sportster. The motorcycle was mildly customized to help give the character more individuality. Modifications included bobbed front and rear fenders, a 21-inch front wheel, and the red gas tank with the eye-over-the-pyramid logo.

No Harley-Davidson logos appeared on the bike, despite the manufacturer's involvement in the show. Harley-Davidson also supplied a Sprint 350 and Rapido 125 for the off-road scenes. *Photofest*

Hollywood "kustomizer" George Barris built this replica 1914 Stutz Bearcat specifically for use in the short-lived TV series *Bearcats!*. The frame was modified from a rectangular Ford truck frame, and the 18-gauge steel body was hand-formed from molds of a real Bearcat. It was powered by a Ford inline six-cylinder truck engine with an automatic transmission and Ford rear end. *John Boyce*

was modified with a sidecar to hold the camera for the moving close-ups.

The road-based Sporty was not capable of any of the rigorous off-road sequences that were frequently part of the story line, so the SS350 and Rapido 125s were used for the off-road stunts and various other stunt riding scenes. A CZ was used for the hill-climb in the pilot movie. There was much speculation about the various bikes used in the series. Despite popular myth, no Japanese bikes were used in the show.

The motorcycle in the show became very popular among cycle enthusiasts, so popular, in fact, that a plastic model kit was offered by MPC, and Harley-Davidson marketed cans of red paint known as "Bronson Red."

Despite being popular with the motorcycle crowd the show never really caught on with the mainstream, and it was too tame to identify with the rebellious culture of the day. It was cancelled after one season.

The bikes from the original pilot were sold off after the crew wrapped production. The motorcycles were returned to Harley-Davidson as part of their agreement to provide bikes, with the exception of one that was destroyed from being repeatedly dropped for sound effects.

Bearcats! (1971 (CBS))
Filmways Productions
Starring Rod Taylor and Dennis Cole

This was a short-lived adventure series remembered mostly by car enthusiasts who were captivated by the car more than the stories.

Set in 1914, *Bearcats!* features Hank Brackett (Rod Taylor) and Johnny Reach (Dennis Cole) as do-gooders for hire driving around the American southwest in their Stutz Bearcat. Their services have no particular fee; instead, they ask their clients for a blank check and then fill in a fair price after the job is done.

Gilbert Metals used actual brass to make the radiator and headlamps to authenticate the appearance of the car. A 40-gallon "Moonspun" gas tank was fitted behind the twin bucket seats. The seats were finished in diamond-tufted red leather. *John Boyce*

Obviously an original Stutz Bearcat would be too fragile for the kinds of action and stunts called for in the scripts. (In one episode the tires were removed so the car could ride on railroads tracks.) Filmways, the production company, hired Hollywood customizer George Barris to build a replica Bearcat for the filming.

Barris started with a Ford truck frame as the base to ensure rigidity. An original Stutz was sourced to model the fenders, hood, and radiator but to the scale of the Ford truck frame.

A 272-ci Ford six-cylinder engine powered the Barris Bearcat, which featured an automatic transmission and heavy-duty Ford rear end. Ansen Automotive Industries was hired to make the retro-looking modern suspension components. Moon Equipment custom-built an aluminum 40-gallon fuel tank, while Lester Tire built the wooden spoke wheels, and gauges for the wooden dashboard came from Stuart-Warner.

Three of these Bearcats were built at a total cost of $85,000. One of the cars has been purchased and restored by a collector in Texas.

Starsky & Hutch (1975–1979 (ABC))

Producer: Spelling-Goldberg Productions
Starring: Paul Michael Glaser, David Soul, Bernie Hamilton, and Antonio Fargas

Starsky & Hutch debuted on ABC in the fall of 1975 back when television shows were only launched in September and went into reruns the following summer. It was a buddy show featuring Paul Michael Glaser as Dave Starsky and David Soul as Ken "Hutch" Hutchinson.

The two were street-smart, plain-clothes detectives working the tough streets of Los Angeles, although the specific city was never really identified. When they weren't battling the bad guys they were battling their boss, Captain Dobey, played by the eternally infuriated Bernie Hamilton.

STARSKY & HUTCH

Glaser and Soul at speed in the Gran Torino from the opening credits of *Starsky & Hutch*. Several *Starsky & Hutch* websites allow you to watch the introduction along with the original theme music.

Rounding out the cast was Antonio Fargas as a shamelessly stereotyped con-man-nightclub-owner and snitch named Huggy Bear.

The unlikely star and symbol of the show quickly emerged in the form of a 1975 Ford Gran Torino sporting a radical white stripe. The tomato-red two-door was the on-screen pride and joy of Detective Starsky, but off-screen the development of the car was far less passionate.

The car was chosen by studio transportation chief George Grenier after Spelling asked him to find a car to fit the bill. Grenier raided the lot of Ford loaner cars and found the two-door to be most suitable. He painted it red (Ford paint code 2B) and added the famous white stripe.

No one could have foreseen the popularity created by the seemingly uncalculated decision, least of all the advertisers. Ironically, Dodge and Chevrolet were sponsors of the show.

Aside from the bold cosmetics, the car had Cragar-slotted disc mag wheels and oversized blackwall tires. Hijacker shock absorbers were put in the rear to give the car the exaggerated stance. Air shocks were also put in the front to help with the aggressive driving stunts.

The rest of the car was factory stock, with a cloth bench seat and automatic transmission shifted from the column.

As an auto enthusiast you viewed the car in the context of A) the show—How can this car be

One of the original cars from the show now owned by a collector in Ohio. Note the stripe runs above the bodyside moulding. Also note the scars at the front of the doors. This is from the doors being thrown open as the car races into the picture. The car has just 8,000 miles on it. *Doug Stevenson*

The original 351-ci engine was replaced with a Ford 460 to give the car more street toughness and enough power to spin the rear wheels. David Soul also asked that the bench seat be replaced with bucket seats, because he did not like sliding into his costar when going around corners. *Doug Stevenson*

Starsky's prized possession when he and his partner are constantly jumping on the roof and running across the hood?—and B) reality—a hulking mid-1970s grocery-getter is cool? Somehow the chemistry worked.

A total of six Gran Torinos were used during the 92 episodes of the show. The Ford in the original pilot, the same car used through the first season, was powered by a 400-ci Ford V-8. The cars from the first season had color-keyed sport mirrors but no body side moldings.

The cars used in the second through fourth seasons were fitted with a 460-ci Ford engine to help add excitement to the tire-squealing chase scenes. The second through fourth season cars also had chrome sport mirrors and body side molding with the stripe running under the molding.

A unique modification came at the request of the two stars. The Torinos used in the second season had a vinyl bench seat and apparently the two actors didn't think having Hutch sliding across the seat into Starsky during fast turns was befitting of their macho characters. To remedy this, bucket seats were put in some of the cars, but unfortunately not all of them. If you watch some of the later episodes closely, you'll see the men get into a car with a bench seat and arrive at their destination sitting in bucket seats.

Nonetheless, the show and the car were so popular that Ford produced a factory Starsky model complete with stripe and mag wheels. A 351 Cleveland engine delivered power to the rear tires of the factory version through a C-6 automatic transmission. Just 1,002 were officially built but there were countless clones. The key to the real McCoy is the PS-122 on the data plate.

Building a factory replica suggested Ford was throwing support behind the show, but at the end of the 1976 model year Ford cancelled Gran Torino production. The studio milked the last four cars through the end of the series and received some help from Ford in the form of spare parts.

After the show was cancelled in 1979 the six cars were sold off or left to languish on the studio backlots. Today some collectors have resurrected the cars. One such collector is Doug Stevenson of Ohio. Doug owns two documented show cars and one of the factory Starsky cars.

Both of Doug's show cars are from the later seasons. The first car has 30,000 miles on the odometer and is covered with dents and scratches from the camera mountings and marks from where the stars would put the ubiquitous flashing light on the roof. It also has bucket seats.

The second car has just 8,000 miles on it, which would indicate it was used for the close-up shots. The door hinges are also sprung from the doors being thrown open as the car screeched to a halt and the actors leapt out to chase the bad guys.

A Starsky Gran Torino recently resurfaced in a music video done by Bare Naked Ladies. That car was a clone created from a 1974 car by Hollywood customizer George Barris.

Just after *Starsky & Hutch* was cancelled, one of the studio cars did have a brief role in another television show that catapulted a 1969 Dodge Charger to even greater fame: *The Dukes of Hazzard.*

The Dukes of Hazzard (1979–1985 [CBS])

Producer: Lou Step Productions and Warner Bros. Television
Starring: John Schneider, Tom Wopat, Catherine Bach, Denver Pile, James Best, and Sorrell Booke

Here we have another car whose image and fame eclipsed that of the stars and even the show itself. The car is, of course, the "Jumpin" *General Lee* from *The Dukes of Hazzard.*

The General, as it was known, was billed as a 1969 Dodge Charger with a 440-ci Magnum V-8 engine and an A-727 automatic transmission. The car was really the only redeeming portion of the show. You just had to tune in each week if only to see the improbable spins, stunts, and jumps that the car performed without so much as a scratch. That, and to see what exiguous attire Catherine Bach was thrust into.

The premise of the show was quite simple. Two brothers, Bo and Luke Duke, played by John Schneider and Tom Wopat respectively, are descendants of an infamous moonshiner living in Hazzard County. Each week the boys are wrongly accused of various ridiculous crimes because they keep thwarting the plans of the crooked mayor and the bumbling sheriff. In order to extricate themselves from trouble, a car chase is required.

During these chases the Charger would perform such stupendous stunts that it was unclear

The Dukes of Hazzard cast leaning on the star attraction, a 1969 Dodge Charger with a 440-ci Magnum V-8, known as the "Jumpin" General Lee. From left to right are Tom Wopat, Sorrell Booke, Catherine Bach, and John Schneider. Photofest

whether the car had a driver or pilot. Aside from fishtailing down dirt roads and using the ubiquitous "bootlegger's turn" to elude the insultingly-stupid pursuers, *the General* was capable of soaring over stalled police cars, small ravines, and full-sized barns, given the proper ramp.

The cars used for the filming received surprisingly few modifications to defy all of Newton's labor. Each car was fitted with a Holley 650 Double Pumper carburetor, headers, stiffer shock absorbers, and helper springs at the rear so the car would remain more rigid during the chases.

The parking brake lock was removed on every car to facilitate the bootlegger's turns.

One car was designated as a "first unit" car and used only for all of the close-ups and beauty shots. It had to be constantly wiped down because there was so much shot on dirt roads.

The first unit car had more stunt doubles than any actor in the history of show business. Over 300 Dodge Chargers perished during the seven seasons of *The Dukes of Hazzard*. The studio bought and stock-piled cars for the express purpose of destroying them in a variety of Dukes

The General Lee with Bo and Luke replacements Coy and Vance Duke in action. Over 300 Dodge Chargers perished during the seven seasons of the Dukes TV series. 1968 and 1970 Chargers were also painted up like *the General* and used for a variety of stunts. *Photofest*

stunts. The cars were purchased, painted, given mag wheels, glass-pack mufflers, and a four-barrel carburetor, and fitted with a roll cage. Once the car was used in a jump it was scrapped, even if the footage was unusable. If a retake was required the stunt drivers would simply get another car. Naturally many parts were cannibalized.

To keep the car level during the various aerial stunts, ballast was added to the trunk to counter the cast-iron V-8 in the nose. For shorter jumps of a few feet, 500 pounds was added, and for longer jumps 1,000 pounds of lead was loaded into the trunk.

The studio had quite an appetite for the Chargers too. As the story goes, the studio was so low on stunt cars at one point that staffers were sent out to solicit drivers in driveways and mall parking lots to sell their Chargers. In a pinch, 1968 and 1970 Chargers were also used.

As famous as *the General* became, it is quite amazing how little thought actually went into the choice of the make and model. Show creator Gy Waldron had already written the part of a late 1960's American musclecar into the original script but did not have a specific car in mind. The name *General Lee* was also already written into the story.

Waldron and executive producer Paul Picard picked the Charger after the studio transportation chief showed them a similar car. Orange was selected simply because it was bright and attention getting. The numbers were put on the door to give it more of a stock-car look. The now politically incorrect Confederate stars and stripes were added to the roof to authenticate that deep-in-the-south feel. The doors were welded shut to further perpetuate the race car look.

The General got the "Dixie" horn at the last minute. According to legend, Picard and Waldron were in Georgia for the shooting of the first episode when they heard a car on the street with a horn that played "Way Down South in the Land of Cotton." After a long pursuit they flagged the

Tom Selleck and the signature Ferrari 308GTS. This is a clear example of how a car was used to help define a character. While the car gives character Thomas Magnum an air of success, the car, in the story, is not actually his but belongs to the owner of the estate he is assigned to keep secure. *Everett Collection*

driver down and bought the horn right out of the car at the side of the road.

In the first episode, where we meet the Dukes and *the General*, we also meet local mechanic "Cooter." The Dukes challenge Cooter to a friendly drag race. As it turns out, Cooter drives a 1976 Ford Gran Torino late of *Starsky and Hutch*, complete with stripe.

Magnum P.I. (1980–1988 [CBS])

Producer: Belisarius Productions, Glen A. Larson Productions, Universal TV
Starring: Tom Selleck, John Hillerman, Roger E. Mosely, and Larry Manetti

Magnum P.I., easily one of the most sugarcoated crime dramas on television, was one of those formula shows that hit on all cylinders. You had action, drama, gorgeous women, beautiful scenery, a hunky leading man, and a Ferrari.

It was the story of a Tom Magnum (Selleck), a private eye guarding the estate of wealthy novelist Robin Masters, who never came home. It just so happened that the estate was a sprawling beachfront mansion in Oahu, Hawaii.

When Magnum wasn't trading barbs with the novelist's manservant, Higgins (John Hillerman), he was out solving crimes with the aid of his two buddies, T. C. (Roger E. Mosley) and Rick (Larry Manetti). The only real grit in this drama was the beach sand.

One of the perks Magnum got for house sitting was the use of a 1980 Ferrari 308GTS that he treated as his own.

Peter Falk and the famous Columbo 1960 Peugeot 403 convertible. *Patrick R. Foster*

Dan Tana in his red 1957 Ford Thunderbird in search of his living room. *Photofest*

The car was chosen to add to the exotic nature of the estate and the location. It also suited the character of Magnum and helped to perpetuate the playboy image. However, there was nothing special about the car. It was not customized or modified, nor did it perform stunts or jumps. In fact, the Ferrari never played a major part in any episode, but it was in every show and synonymous with Selleck's character. It was also featured repeatedly in the opening credits.

During the first five years of the show, Robin Masters would "appear" as a voice on the telephone. The voice was that of Orson Welles. It is a bit incongruous to think of Welles in his later years getting in and out of a Ferrari.

Roll Call: Other TV Cars

The Saint (1962–1968)
Roger Moore is a detective in a white Volvo P1800. When the feature film of the same name was made in 1997, Volvo recognized Hollywood's power of promotion and handed the keys to a swoopy new C70 coupe to Val Kilmer.

The Munsters (CBS 1964–1966)

A sitcom about misfit monsters trying to fit into society. Barris built two great hot rods to go with the series: the Munsters' Koach and Grandpa's Dragula. The coach was seen in the closing credits, and both cars are prominently featured in the 1966 feature film *Munster, Go Home*.

Get Smart (NBC 1965–1970)

Don Adams parodies a Bondian spy character. He drives Opel GTs, Karmann Ghias, and Sunbeam Alpines, but all are sans Bond-style gadgets.

My Mother the Car (NBC 1965–1966)

Jerry Van Dyke talks to his mother who has been reincarnated in the form of a 1928 Porter (actually a 1925 Model T touring car with a created "Porter" grille).

The Avengers (ABC 1965–1969)

Proper Patrick Macnee and leather-clad Diana Rigg are tongue-in-cheek British spies in a 1935 Bentley.

Batman (ABC 1966–1968)

This short-lived but immensely popular camp series starring Adam West and Burt Ward created one of the most famous cars in the world. The *Batmobile* was created by George Barris based on styling cues from the 1955 Lincoln Futura show car.

Hawaii Five-O (CBS 1968–1980)

Jack Lord fights crime on the Big Island with a fleet of Fords and Mercurys. His own car was a triple-black 1968 Mercury Parklane.

Columbo (NBC-ABC 1971–1990)

The classic rumpled detective, played by Peter Falk, with his rumpled 1960 Peugeot 403 convertible.

Banacek (NBC 1972–1974)

George Peppard stars as a Boston-based bounty hunter in a chauffeur-driven Darrin-bodied Packard.

The Rockford Files (NBC 1974–1980)

Beleaguered private eye James Garner drives a bronze Pontiac Firebird while solving crimes from his Malibu trailer. Each season he got a new car—perhaps he knew something about leasing? Garner was actually a very accomplished driver and was able to do the patented 180-degree "Rockford turn."

Vega$ (ABC 1978–1981)

Every guy's dream—to be a highly compensated private eye (Robert Urich as Dan Tana) in Las Vegas with Judy Landers as your secretary and the ability to park your 1957 Ford Thunderbird in your living room.

B.J. and the Bear (NBC 1979–1981)

An hour-long series featuring trucker B.J. (Greg Evigan) and Bear, B.J.'s pet chimpanzee. The pair become entangled in a series of misadventures as they travel around the country in their big rig.

Knight Rider (NBC 1982–1986)

Campy action-adventure series starring David Hasselhoff as a problem-solver for hire and his sidekick—a talking 1983 Pontiac Trans Am known as KITT. Trick bits on the car were done by Barris.

The A-Team (NBC 1983–1987)

George Peppard and Mr. T are Vietnam veterans running from the law and doing good deeds, with a customized GMC van as their base of operations.

Miami Vice (NBC 1984–1989)

Ultra-stylish 1980s cop show set in sunny Miami. Don Johnson and Philip Michael Thomas thwart drug smugglers in expensive clothes and a faux Ferrari Daytona Spyder. The car was actually a kit-car based on a Corvette chassis. Late in the series they switched to a white Ferrari Testarossa.

Spenser: For Hire (ABC 1985–1988)

Robert Urich is a Boston-based private eye in a 1966 Ford Mustang Fastback. His smooth, enigmatic sidekick drives a BMW 633 CSI.

Viper (NBC 1994)

Dopey short-lived saga of crime fighters in a morphing Dodge Viper.

Nash Bridges (CBS 1996–present)

Cop Don Johnson trades pastel suits, T-shirts, Ferraris, and Miami for vests, San Francisco, and a yellow 1971 (some say 1970) Plymouth 'Cuda 426 Hemi convertible, which is, of course, a fake, since there were only seven such cars ever made, and each remaining car is essentially irreplaceable.

Index

24 Hours of Le Mans, 76, 90
A View to a Kill, 26
Adam, Ken, 16, 90
Agajanian, Jerry, 48
Alamo Car Museum, 60
Alfa Romeo GTV, 26
AMC Matador, 25, 26
American Graffiti, 9, 57, 60, 62–65
American Motors Corporation, 24, 26
Amon, Chris, 77
Ansen Automotive Industries, 117
Aston Martin (company), 16, 10, 23
Aston Martin DB4, 43
Aston Martin DB5, 9, 13, 16, 17, 19, 20, 21, 29, 32, 36, 44
Aston Martin DBS, 24, 25
Attwood, Richard, 84
Austin Healey (company), 10
Austin Powers: International Man of Mystery, 55
Austin-Healey, 87
B. J. and the Bear, 126
Back to the Future, 7, 11, 98–100
Back to the Future, Part II, 7
Back to the Future, Part III, 7
Balchowski, Max, 40
Bandini, Lorenzo, 77
Banecek, 10, 126
Bare Naked Ladies, 120
Baretta, 10
Barris Bearcat, 117
Barris, George, 9, 69, 101, 103, 113, 116, 117, 120, 126
Baskerville, Gray, 68
Batman Returns, 55
Batman, 55, 103, 126
Batmobile, 9, 103, 104
Bearcats!, 116, 117
Bell Labs, 76
Bell, Derek, 84
Bentley, 16, 25, 126
Bikers, 57
Bill Young's Precision Driving Team, 50
Billy Bike, 59
Black Beauty, 103, 104, 107, 109
Black Moon Rising, 85
BMW (company), 10, 30, 32, 35, 36, 37
BMW 633 CSI, 36
BMW 750iL, 30, 32, 33, 34, 35, 36
BMW R1200, 34, 36
BMW Z3, 30, 32, 37
BMW Z8, 35, 37
Bobby Deerfield, 71, 85
Bond, James, 9, 12–22
Bondurant, Bob, 77
Bonnier, Joakim, 77
Boss, Cliff, 58
Boyce, Tommy, 111
Brabham, Jack, 77
Broccoli, Albert, 87
Brosnan, Pierce, 13, 29, 30

BSA 10, 20
BSA 650 Lightning, 20
Buford, Gordon, 92
Buick Apollo, 92
Bullitt, 39–42
C.C. and Company, 10
Cage, Nicolas, 50
Caine, Michael, 42
California Department of Motor Vehicles, 96
Captain America, 58, 59
Carpenter, John, 95
Casino Royale, 16
Caulfield, Dale, 68
Chaplin, Charlie, 9
Chapouris, Pete, 68
Chevrolet 150, 60, 64
Chevrolet Bel Air, 63
Chevrolet Camaro, 62, 96
Chevrolet Corvette, 41, 84
Chevrolet Impala, 10, 55
Chitty Chitty Bang Bang, 87–90
Christine, 11, 86, 87, 94–97
Chrysler Imperial, 104
Citroen 2CV, 26
Cobb, Ron, 99
Cobra, 55
Columbia Pictures, 96
Columbo, 10, 124, 126
Competition Engineering, 60
Connery, Sean, 13, 17, 18, 23–25
Coppola, Francis Ford, 69
Corvette Summer, 56, 57, 69
Crombac, Jabby, 83
CZ, 113, 116
Dallas, 8
Darrin-bodied Packard, 10, 126
Datsun Z car, 8
Days of Thunder, 71, 85
Death Race 2000, 85
DeLorean, 7, 98–100
DeLorean, John Z., 6, 7, 98, 112
Diamonds Are Forever, 24
Dirty Mary, Crazy Larry, 69
Disney, Walt, 92
Dodge Challenger, 61, 62
Dodge Charger 440 Magnum, 39–42
Dodge Charger R/T 440, 69
Dodge Charger, 121, 122
Dodge Monaco, 69
Dr. No, 13, 16
Drag Strip Girl, 11
Driving Miss Daisy, 10
Duel, 8
Duesenberg, 10
Easy Rider, 10, 57–61, 113
Edwards, Blake, 71
Ekins, Bud, 40, 42
Eleanor, 48, 46–49
Elford, Vic, 84
Emergency, 8
Every Which Way But Loose, 8

Falcon Crest, 8
Fangio, Juan Manuel, 77
Fantasy, 87–101
Ferrari 250GT Spyder, 101
Ferrari 275 GTB, 69
Ferrari 308GTS, 10, 123, 125
Ferrari 355 GTS, 20, 32
Ferrari 512LM, 82, 83, 85
Ferrari Daytona Spyder kit car, 10, 103, 126
Ferrari Testarossa, 126
Ferris Bueller's Day Off, 101
Fiat (company), 43
Filmtrix, Inc., 99
Fireball 500, 11, 69
Fleming, Ian, 13, 87
Fonda, Peter, 57, 58
For Your Eyes Only, 26
Ford five-window hot rod, 63, 64
Ford Gran Torino, 10, 118–120, 123
Ford GT40, 76, 82, 84, 90
Ford Motor Company, 25
Ford Mustang 390 GT, 39–42
Ford Mustang fastback, 126
Ford Mustang Mach I, 25
Ford Mustang, 19, 21, 46
Ford Skyliner, 20
Ford three-window coupe hot rod, 68
Ford Thunderbird, 63, 69, 125, 126
Ford, 6, 7
Frankenheimer, John 71, 76, 79
Frobe, Gert, 18
From Russia With Love, 16
Gale, Bob, 99
Garner, James, 79
Get Smart, 10, 126
Ghostbusters, 101
Gilbert Metals, 117
Ginther, Richie, 77
GMC, 8
GoldenEye, 13, 20, 29, 31
Goldfinger, 9, 13, 16–18, 23
Goldfinger, Auric, 18
Gone in 60 Seconds remake, 49
Gone in 60 Seconds, 39, 44, 46–50
Graham, Jim, 7, 50
Grand Prix motor racing, 76
Grand Prix, 9, 76–81
Greased Lightning, 85
Green Hornet, 103–109
Gregory, Masten, 84
Grenier, George, 118
Gulf-Porsche 917K, 70, 71, 81, 82, 84, 85
Gumball Rally, 85
Gurney, Dan, 77

Halicki, Denice, 48, 49
Halicki, Toby, 46–49
Hall, Tex, 59
Hannibal Twin 8, 73–76
Hardcastle and McCormick, 8
Harley-Davidson 883 Sportster, 113, 114
Harley-Davidson Panhead, 58
Harley-Davidson Rapido 125, 113, 116
Harley-Davidson Sprint 350, 113, 116
Harley-Davidson (company), 57, 113, 116
Harry O, 10, 87
Hart, Bobby, 111
Hawaii Five-O, 126
Herbie Goes Bananas, 92, 94
Herbie Goes to Monte Carlo, 91, 94
Herbie Rides Again, 91, 94
Herbie the Love Bug, 94
Herbie, 90
Hickman, Bill, 41
Hill, Graham, 77
Hill, Phil, 77
Hooper, 69
Hopper, Dennis, 57
Horwitz, Howie, 68
Hot Rod Gang, 10
Hot Rod Girl, 10
Hot Rod Hullabaloo, 10
Hot Rod, 10
Hot Rods to Hell, 10
Hudson Hornet, 10
Hulme, Dennis, 77
Huyck, William, 63
HVM, 85
It's a Mad, Mad, Mad, Mad World, 100
Jabouille, Jean-Pierre, 84
Jacobs, Jim "Jake", 68
Jaguar XKE Series I, 43
Jaguar XKE Series II, 55
Jaws, 8
Jeffries, Dean, 103, 104, 106–109, 111–113
Jim Russell Driving School, 78–81
Jones, Parnelli, 48
Jumpin' General Lee, 120, 121
Karmann Ghia, 10, 126
Katz, Gloria, 63
Keaton, Buster, 9
Keystone Cops, 9, 39
King of the Mountain, 85
King, Malcolm, 85
King, Steven, 87, 94, 95
KITT, 11, 126
Knight Rider, 8, 11, 126
Korkes, Richard, 56, 69
Kovacs, Laszlo, 57, 59
Kowalski, 61
Laurel and Hardy, 7

Lazenby, George, 23, 24
Le Mans, 6, 71, 77, 81–85
Lelouch, Claude, 69
Leslie Special, 72–74, 76
Lincoln Futura Concept Car, 9, 126
Live and Let Die, 26
Loftin, Carey, 61, 62
Lola T70 IIIB, 84, 85
Lotus (company), 10
Lotus Esprit, 13, 26–30
Lotus Formula 3, 80
Lucas, George, 57, 63, 64
Mad Max, 101
Magnum P.I., 10, 123, 125
Main, Ron,11
Man with the Golden Gun, 24
Mann, Alan, 90
Mann, Dave, 11
McLaren, Bruce, 77
McQueen, Steve, 6, 39, 40, 70, 71, 77, 81–85
Mercury Parklane, 126
Miami Vice, 10, 103, 126
Mini Cooper, 43, 45
Mitchell, Bill, 51
Model Productions Corporation, 111, 112
Monkeemobile, 103, 108, 109, 111–113
Moore, Roger, 13, 26, 27
More American Graffiti, 65
Motorcycles, 85, 113–116
Movin' On, 8
Munsters, 126
My Mother the Car, 11, 126
My Three Sons, 11
Nash Bridges, 10, 126
National Lampoon's Vacation, 27, 30
Needham, Hal, 7, 50, 51
Never Say Never Again, 16, 25
Octopussy, 26
Oddjob, 18
On Any Sunday, 85
On Her Majesty's Secret Service, 23
Opel GT, 10, 126
Packard (company), 10
Packard, 7
Parkes, Mike, 77
Partridge Family, 11
Paul, Eddie, 55
Perry Submarine Company, 27, 30
Petitclerc, Denne Bart, 83
Peugeot 403, 124, 126
Peugeot, 10
Pike, Kevin, 99
Planes, Trains, and Automobiles, 11, 101
Plymouth Barracuda 426 Hemi, 102, 126

Plymouth Barracuda, 10, 69
Plymouth Belvedere, 96
Plymouth Fury, 11, 95, 96
Plymouth Savoy, 96
Pontiac (company), 50, 60
Pontiac Firebird, 10, 126
Pontiac GTO, 103, 111–113
Pontiac Trans Am Special Edition, 50, 51
Pontiac Trans Am Turbo V-6, 52, 53
Pontiac Trans Am, 7, 8, 11, 53, 69, 126
Pontiac, 7
Porsche 356, 85, 93
Porsche 908, 83
Porsche 911, 84
Porsche 917LH, 84
Porsche, 6
Porter, 11, 103, 126
Probert, Andy, 99
Races, Chases, and Crashes, 11
Racing, 70–85
Redman, Brian, 84
Rendezvous, 69
Revson, Peter, 77
Rindt, Jochen, 77
Rod & Custom magazine, 68
Rolls-Royce Phantom III Sedanca de Ville, 18, 19
Russell, Jim, 80
Russell, Peter, 80
Ruth, Richard, 60
Sakata, Harold, 18
Schinella, John, 51
Shaguar, 53
Shelby Cobra, 76
Shelby Mustang GT 500, 38, 50
Shoppe, James, 56, 69
Siffert, Jo, 77, 84
Simon, David, 76
Slotemake, Bob, 84
Smokey and the Bandit II, 8, 11, 53
Smokey and the Bandit III, 53
Smokey and the Bandit, 7, 39, 50–54
Smokey Mountain Car Museum, 20
Solar Productions, 84
Southern, Terry, 57
Spenser: For Hire, 126
Spy, 26
SSXR, 69
Star Cars Museum, 90
Starsky & Hutch, 10, 117–120, 123
Stears, John, 16, 18, 20, 23
Stevenson, Doug, 120
Stutz Bearcat, 116, 117
Sunbeam Alpine, 10
Tomorrow Never Dies, 31–34
Toteff, George, 111
Toyota (company), 23

The Car, 87, 101
The Devil's Hairpin, 11
The Driver, 55
The Dukes of Hazzard, 120–123
The French Connection, 39
The Good Guys and the Bad Guys, 76
The Great Race, 71–76
The Green Helmet, 11
The Italian Job, 42–44
The Love Bug, 11, 91
The Monkees, 109–113
The Munsters, 126
The Racers, 11, 85
The Rockford Files, 8, 10, 126
The Saint, 125
The Spy Who Loved Me, 13, 26–28
The Three Stooges, 8
The Sting, 10
The Wild One, 10
The World Is Not Enough, 35–37
The Yellow Rolls-Royce, 100
Thelma & Louise, 69
Then Came Bronson, 11, 113–116
Thomas Flyer, 71, 73
Thorndyke Special, 92
Thunderball, 9, 19, 25, 69
THX 1138, 63, 64
THX 138, 64
Tomorrow Never Dies, 31–34
Toteff, George, 111
Toyota (company), 23
Toyota 2000 GT, 22, 23
Trintignant, Maurice, 69
Triumph motorcycles, 10
Tucker: The Man and His Dream, 69
TV shows, 103–126
Two Lane Blacktop, 57, 60, 64, 65
Universal Studios, 111
Vanishing Point, 60–62
Vega$, 126
Viper, 126
Viva Las Vegas, 11, 71, 85
Volkswagen Beetle, 11, 92
Volvo C70, 125
Volvo P1800, 125
Waldron, Guy, 122
Wangers, Jim, 111, 112
Warner Brothers, 72, 73
Webber Motor Car Company, 71
Wet Nellie, 28
Winning, 11, 85
Yamaha XJ650, 26
You Only Live Twice, 22, 23
Zemeckis, Robert, 98, 99

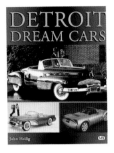
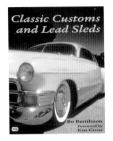

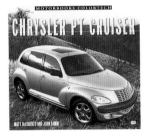
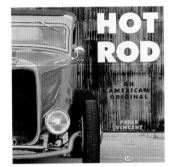
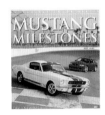

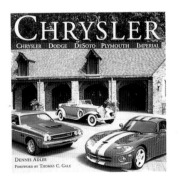